THE eBay
BILLIONAIRES'
CLUB

THE eBay BILLIONAIRES' CLUB

Exclusive Secrets
for Building an Even Bigger and More Profitable Online Business

AMY JOYNER

1807
WILEY
2007
BICENTENNIAL

John Wiley & Sons, Inc.

Published by John Wiley & Sons, Inc., Hoboken, New Jersey.
Published simultaneously in Canada.

Wiley Bicentennial Logo: Richard J. Pacifico.

For general information on our other products and services or for technical support, please contact our Customer Care Department within the United States at (800) 762-2974, outside the United States at (317) 572-3993 or fax (317) 572-4002.

Wiley also publishes its books in a variety of electronic formats. Some content that appears in print may not be available in electronic books. For more information about Wiley products, visit our web site at www.wiley.com.

Library of Congress Cataloging-in-Publication Data:
Joyner, Amy.
    The eBay billionaires' club : exclusive secrets for building an even bigger and more profitable online business / Amy Joyner.
        p.   cm.
Includes index.
ISBN 978-0-470-05574-8 (cloth)
    1. eBay (Firm) 2. Internet auctions. 3. Businesspeople. 4. Success in business. 5. Electronic commerce. I. Title.
HF5478.J688 2007
658.8'7—dc22

                                                                    2006037896

Printed in the United States of America.

10   9   8   7   6   5   4   3   2   1

To Jackson and Bruce,
who fill my life with joy, laughter, and love

CONTENTS

THE eBaY
BILLIONAIRES'
CLUB

INTRODUCTION

Of the millions of eBay sellers online today, only a handful qualify for membership in a special club consisting of the legendary auction site's cream-of-the-crop merchants. Collectively, those fortunate enough to join the ranks of this club sell more than $1 billion in merchandise each year and are responsible for more than 70 million annual transactions. They know how to find the best inventory, price right for the most effective sale, and keep customers coming back again and again.

Now, for the first time ever, members of this elite organization—what I call The eBay Billionaires' Club—show you how to build your own highly successful eBay business. On each information-packed page, you'll discover proven and tested strategies you can use to help propel your eBay business into the major leagues. You'll also uncover insider secrets from those who've truly perfected the art of online selling.

Specifically, each online entrepreneur featured in *The eBay Billionaires' Club* is affiliated with the Professional eBay Sellers Alliance, also known as PeSA. This is the world's largest trade organization dedicated to eBay professionals. The association's strict membership requirements mandate that you must already have a thriving business—and therefore documented success—in order to join. Now, their incredible knowledge is at your disposal.

Amazingly, there are some who still think of eBay as nothing more than an online flea market. That kind of mind-set is so outdated. In recent years, the online trading community that Pierre Omidyar founded in 1995 has blossomed into one of the world's most robust marketplaces. The site fuels billions of dollars in e-commerce every year as buyers and sellers negotiate deals for all sorts of merchandise, including items once found only in the world's most exclusive and expensive retail stores.

During its decade-long history, eBay has made great evolutionary strides. It has transformed itself into a sophisticated marketplace populated by professional merchants with individual sales that quite often total in the millions of dollars annually. Nearly a quarter of all Internet purchases occur on eBay—to the tune of about $44 billion annually, according to the most recent tally. In all, eBay reports 212 million users worldwide, 105 million items for sale at any given time, 6 million new listings each day, and completed sales of roughly $1,590 every second. Given those statistics, it's no wonder that more and more Americans (and an increasing number of global Internet surfers, as well) are turning to eBay as a way to launch their own part-time, or even full-time, businesses. According to eBay, more than two million people sell enough merchandise on eBay for it to have a significant impact on their bottom line. While there are plenty of folks who dabble on eBay just now and then, nearly three-quarters of a million members rank eBay as their primary or secondary source of income, according to a survey conducted on behalf of the company.

In *The eBay Billionaires' Club*, you will read the stories of 12 professional eBay merchants who recognized a great business opportunity on the Internet and pursued it—some at great personal financial risk. In every case, the gamble has paid off. Many of the merchants profiled in these pages have achieved the vaunted Titanium PowerSeller status, the zenith of success on eBay. (To qualify for that distinction, an eBayer must sell more than $150,000 in merchandise on the site every month.) Many have used eBay as the foundation for a profitable online empire generating millions of dollars in annual revenues on multiple Internet e-commerce sites.

There are some powerful lessons to be learned from these entrepreneurs, whose experience truly runs the gamut. In the end, what they all have in common is that they started small—and some have purposely decided to stay that way. I made a conscious decision to focus on such companies for this book, because chances are you'll see yourself through each of these stories, especially if you're just starting out. You'll quickly discover that eBay success really is within your reach, because every person in this book also began at the very bottom and worked their way up the ladder of success. What's more, a number of them have achieved incredible growth in a relatively short period of time, which should motivate you to stop thinking about your idea and get started on the road to becoming a member of this elite club yourself.

Throughout *The eBay Billionaires' Club*, you'll meet several young CEOs, including Adam Hersh of Adam Hersh Auctions and Dan Yen of Movie Mars. All started selling on eBay right out of college and realized that doing so was more lucrative than finding a job in their respective majors. The book also includes more senior members, such as Connie Gray of Estate Treasure by Byrum, David Yaskulka of Blueberry Boutique, Anthony Roberts of AACS Autographs, and Robert Walzer of Forklift Deals, all of whom turned to eBay after leaving careers in completely different fields. At the same time, you'll discover how long-established companies such as Gem Stone King turned to eBay as a way to take their existing bricks-and-mortar businesses to a whole new level.

The companies featured in this book are as unique as the people running them. Some start the bidding on every eBay auction at 99 cents, while others are more conservative in their pricing. Some stock their eBay stores with merchandise, while others sell exclusively through auctions. Some sell merchandise on consignment, while others purchase their inventory outright. But they also have a number of things in common, which you will learn about as we go along.

The members of *The eBay Billionaires' Club* sell a variety of merchandise: autographed memorabilia, movie posters, men's ties and clothing, model trains, antiques, computer equipment, designer merchandise, forklifts, fine jewelry, collectible coins, consumer electronics, and outfits for little girls. However, each seller has enjoyed great success after building his or her online businesses from the ground up.

The eBay Billionaires' Club is different from other how-to guides about eBay in that each chapter includes a lengthy question-and-answer interview with the featured seller. This allows you to eavesdrop on my exclusive conversations with these merchants as they share their stories and hard-earned tips for succeeding on eBay.

In their own words, the featured sellers reveal such things as:

- Strategies for getting started on eBay.
- Deciding what to sell.
- Sourcing inventory.
- Handling growth.
- Shipping goods most efficiently.
- Cultivating and managing international sales.
- Researching the eBay marketplace.
- Establishing important relationships with offshore manufacturers.
- Minimizing eBay fees and other business costs.
- Managing employees.
- Attracting customers to eBay auctions.
- Using eBay to drive traffic to your own e-commerce web sites.
- And much more.

Each profile contains a series of "PowerPointer" tips, highlighting various techniques that can be applied to your own eBay business right away. In addition, *The eBay Billionaires' Club* includes several sections that you're sure to find useful as you build your own eBay business. Be sure to check out the one titled "Fifty Secrets of *The eBay Billionaires' Club*," which summarizes the best business tips espoused by those featured throughout the preceding chapters. The book also contains a handy list of resources that these storied merchants have used to propel their online businesses.

Though their paths to success and their business models vary greatly, the members of *The eBay Billionaires' Club* all share two very important traits: First, their online companies, in addition to generating impressive revenues, are profitable. That's a claim that many American businesses—both large and small—can't make. Second, the members of *The eBay Billionaires' Club* have all used networking to great advantage, largely by availing themselves of the many brainstorming opportunities made possible through their membership in PeSA.

If you are serious about selling on eBay, I recommend that you consider joining PeSA (even if you're not big enough for full membership, you can apply for the associate program), as well as any other networking groups out there that can help you build your business and grow your online sales to their fullest potential. You never know: I may be contacting you next to share your eBay success story! To learn more about PeSA and the various membership requirements, visit www.gopesa.com.

You will find a host of business-building resources on eBay, and the community forums and user groups are among the most worthwhile. There, you'll meet other, more experienced eBay sellers who may be willing to mentor you or offer advice that will make your online business stronger. There are literally hundreds of eBay user groups, each targeted to a specific niche. You'll find groups comprised of PowerSellers, people with full-time jobs who sell part-time on eBay, trading assistants, eBay store owners, new eBay sellers, stay-at-home parents, antiques merchants, and the list goes on. Check out http://hub.ebay.com/community to learn how to connect with other eBay users who can help you navigate the site and discover how to sell in this dynamic online marketplace. Don't be afraid to ask for help and to post queries to other eBay users who have already been there, done that. I think you'll find that most of them are very willing to offer advice and to pay forward the mentoring they received as eBay amateurs.

We'll talk more about networking throughout the book. Right now, however, let's get started. Get your highlighters out and fasten your seat belts for a journey that will put you on the road to building your own million-dollar—or perhaps even billion-dollar—eBay business!

ESSENTIAL STEPS FOR
GETTING STARTED ON eBAY

Because I know readers come to this information from all different experience levels, I want to first start off with the basics you need to know in order to get your business started on eBay. Those of you already up and running can certainly skip ahead to the first profile, if you'd like. But this information may still serve as a helpful refresher even for the most experienced online merchant. I've adapted this information from my book *The eBay Millionaire* (John Wiley & Sons, 2005), which features the strategies and techniques of eBay's largest and most successful Titanium PowerSellers. I highly recommend that you check this book out as well, if you already haven't, to get more great ideas on how to stand out from the crowd in what is increasingly becoming a highly competitive marketplace.

Step 1: Start off as a customer. Many of the merchants featured in this book got started as customers on the eBay site. Seeing eBay through the eyes of a buyer serves three purposes: It allows you to become more familiar with how the site works, enables you to build up your feedback score, and gives you the opportunity to check out the competition. Along the way, you'll learn some valuable strategies on how to more effectively sell and offer good customer service. For instance, if someone fails to respond and answer your e-mail queries, you'll know to do a better job in getting back to customers yourself. Or perhaps you'll discover a more effective way to package your goods based on what you learn from an item you receive for yourself in the mail.

Step 2: If you don't already have an eBay user ID, register for one. Anyone can browse through the millions of items for auction on eBay, but only registered members may buy or sell on the site. (You must be at least 18 years old to register.)

Registering to become a member of the eBay community is simple, and it doesn't cost a thing. From the eBay home page at www.ebay.com, click on the "Register" link at the top of the page. You'll be prompted to enter your name, address, telephone number, and e-mail address. Then, you'll choose your eBay user ID, which is the name that all your customers will know you by, and select a password that will protect access to your account.

Pick a name that will be easy for your future customers to remember. If you plan to expand your business, don't choose a user ID that will hamstring you in the future. To complete the registration process, you'll have to read and agree to eBay's user agreement and privacy policy and confirm your e-mail address. Then, you're ready to sell.

Step 3: Find some merchandise to sell. There's a market for just about everything on eBay, as you'll learn by reading the profiles in this book. But start off small before going overboard in buying merchandise. Test the marketplace by putting one or two items up for bid initially. That way, you can get a taste of the whole eBay selling process—from posting to shipping—without getting overwhelmed or spending a lot of money.

Step 4: Buy a digital camera. To successfully sell on eBay, you need to include a photograph with each auction listing. Photographs are not required, but you'll attract more bidders by using them.

If you plan to do a lot of selling on eBay, your best bet is to invest in a digital camera. That way, you don't have to wait until you finish a roll of film to post your auctions. Instead, you can plug the digital camera into your computer and transfer the images to your hard drive in seconds.

When buying a digital camera for eBay, look for one that has image capture capabilities of at least 2 megapixels. These days, most digital cameras on the market offer much higher resolution than that. Also choose a camera with macro capabilities. This will enable you to take close-up pictures without losing focus or distorting the image. You may also want to invest in special lighting and neutral-colored backgrounds to give your auction photographs a professional look.

Step 5: Photograph your items. Once you've settled on what you want to sell, take pictures to accompany your auction listings. Photograph your items in a well-lit and uncluttered area to ensure that you get the sharpest images. Depending on what you're selling, you may want to take multiple photographs from various angles. If there are any special markings or flaws on your item, take close-up photographs of those. Then, transfer the images to your computer and, if necessary, spend some time cropping and cleaning up the images.

Step 6: Research your selling options. Before listing an item, visit eBay and use the web site's built-in search engine to see if similar items are up for auction. This way, you'll be able determine which of eBay's thousands of categories your item fits in.

You'll also discover what similar items are selling for—and whether they are selling well. EBay charges sellers for each auction they place. If you find that there are a thousand items identical to yours for sale and none have bids, you may want to rethink that auction. Instead, choose to sell something that has higher demand or is in shorter supply so you won't lose money.

Step 7: Begin preparing your auction listing. From the eBay home page, click on the "Sell" button. You'll first need to decide whether you want to allow shoppers to bid on your item through an online auction or whether you want to sell it at a fixed price to the first eBay user who chooses to "Buy It Now." (Later, once you become a more experienced eBay merchant, you may want to open an eBay store.)

Next, you'll be prompted for your eBay user ID and password. Once you enter that data, the page advances to the auction listing form.

Step 8: Pick a category. Your next step is to select an eBay category to sell in. There are about 24,000 listed on the site, so choose carefully, because many shoppers browse for merchandise by category. EBay does allow sellers to list items in two different categories. Doing so boosts bids by 18 percent and the final sale price by 17 percent, according to eBay, but you will have to pay an additional listing fee if you choose this option.

Step 9: Write a customer-grabbing headline. Once you've determined which category to sell in, you must write a title for your auction. You'll want a title or headline that's informative and packed with keywords.

Most shoppers go to eBay looking for a particular item, and they'll search using brand names and other keywords, so it's important to include as much specific descriptive information as possible in your title.

Step 10: Write the description. Once you've given your auction a title, it's time to describe your item. The item description is your chance to sell your merchandise to eBay's vast buying public, so be as thorough as possible.

EBay bidders want details, so tell them as much as you know. But be honest: Don't omit information about defects in an attempt to drive the selling price higher. If an item is well worn, chipped, or torn, don't try to pass it off as new out of the box. If you lie about an item, your feedback rating will likely suffer and you'll lose business in the future.

Finally, avoid hyperbole—the used-car salesman approach doesn't sit well with eBay buyers. It's also a good idea to set out your payment or shipping terms in your item description. Let your bidders know if you'll accept checks, money orders, credit cards, PayPal, or some other online payment method, and how much you charge for shipping.

Step 11: Set your price. Now you must decide the starting price for your auction. Many eBay Titanium PowerSellers recommend starting auctions low, at a penny or 99 cents. This saves you money on listing fees, and it also attracts more bargain-seeking bidders.

But if you start an auction cheap, your item may sell for that price if only one person bids. Are you willing to take that risk?

To protect yourself, you may opt to place a reserve on your auction. A reserve is the minimum price you're willing to accept. If no bid matches or tops your reserve, you don't have to sell the item. EBay assesses an extra fee for reserve price auctions.

Step 12: Pick your time period. Decide whether you want your auction to end in one, three, five, seven, or ten days. (You'll pay an extra fee for a ten-day auction.)

Most eBay auctions last for a week, but you may not begin to see heavy bidding until the final day or even the final few minutes of the auction.

Step 13: Attach your pictures. By this point, you're almost finished with your listing. But you've got to put the icing on the cake. From the online listing tool, follow eBay's instructions to attach photographs to your auction, though be aware of the costs based on the number and size of your pictures.

Step 14: Choose additional listing options. To improve the visibility of your auction, you may pay more to customize it. You can choose to have your item title appear in bold text, or add a gallery image to your auction. A gallery image is a small picture that appears in the eBay category listings and search pages. It allows customers to see what you have for sale without clicking on your auction.

Step 15: Select shipping and payment terms. Next, eBay will prompt you to choose how you want to be paid for your item. You'll check off boxes to designate these preferences. If you decide to accept checks or money orders, you should tell buyers where to mail them. (You may have already included this information in your item description, but it's a good idea to repeat it so bidders are clearly informed of your auction terms.)

You'll also check off boxes to indicate where you'll ship items. You can choose to ship worldwide, to the United States only, or to various other regions around the world.

In this step, you can also specify how much you'll charge for shipping and which carriers you'll use, or you may omit those details.

Before bidding, most eBay users like to know what their total cost will be, including shipping. Therefore, it's a good idea to include that price in your auction listing. Otherwise, you can integrate eBay's shipping calculator in your auction ad.

To determine delivery costs, bidders enter their zip codes into the shipping calculator. Using the zip code and size and weight data that you provide when creating the auction, the calculator computes a shipping estimate.

Step 16: Preview your auction. Before your auction goes live, eBay gives you a chance to preview the listing and make any changes. Proofread carefully and check your prices because once you start receiving bids your ability to make changes to the auction listing is limited.

Step 17: Post your auction. When you've determined that the auction ad is perfect, hit the "Submit Listing" button. As soon as you do, your item will be posted on eBay, and you'll have access to a marketplace that is more than 120 million people strong and growing every year.

1

Anthony Roberts

AACS Autographs

Some days, Anthony Roberts misses his old job.

Until about two years ago, he was a high school history and social studies teacher. He also coached the varsity basketball team. Roberts particularly enjoyed the opportunity to mentor teenagers and help them shape their futures. But his day job eventually got in the way of the plan Roberts had for his own future—finding success as an online entrepreneur. So, he decided to quit teaching in order to pursue a more lucrative career on eBay.

Roberts first started tinkering on the site around 1995, when he and his wife decided they were ready to start a family. They knew having kids was an expensive undertaking, and started exploring ways to supplement their income.

Roberts found the perfect solution packed away in his childhood memories.

When Roberts was a child, his father was head of security at Samuel Goldwyn's movie studio. Roberts grew up around celebrities, and managed to amass quite a collection of autographs of the rich and famous.

For the sake of his growing family, Roberts decided to begin selling off that collection, choosing to market the items on a niche online auction site. Within two years, he moved over to eBay, which by then was a behemoth in the Web-based collectibles trade.

"In the early days of eBay it was much easier to make a lot of money because there wasn't as much competition, and eBay was really all about collectibles," Roberts says. "Things would just sell for ridiculous prices. It was easy money back in those days."

Maintaining an eBay business now isn't quite as easy, but Roberts and his wife are doing rather well for themselves. They've established their company, AACS Autographs, as a trustworthy and credible source of autographed memorabilia.

Although Roberts' personal collection is long gone, he now auctions off thousands of autographed vintage memorabilia—signed photographs, trading cards, baseballs, jerseys, and other collectibles—using the eBay user ID aacsautographs.

AACS Autographs, which is based in central Iowa, has become one of the largest autograph memorabilia dealers in the world both on eBay and beyond. The company has completed more than 100,000 online transactions, selling more than 200,000 items, since making the leap to eBay almost a decade ago. AACS maintains about 2,000 listings on eBay at any given time, and revenues are growing by 20 percent to 25 percent a year.

The hard work in running the site has paid off for Roberts and his family in more ways than one. Financial success has allowed them to hire help, freeing Roberts and his wife to take more time off from the business.

In the following interview, Roberts shares some of the strategies he used to build a big eBay business, including pouring most early profits back into inventory and operations. He also talks about how he built a reputation as an honest purveyor of authentic goods in a merchandise category that is rife with fraud, which will be of special interest to those of you considering selling antiques and collectibles online. Finally, he offers advice on how the right equipment and proper listing upgrades can help eBay sellers bring products to market faster while commanding higher prices.

Joyner: It seems that every eBay seller has a story about an item that sold for more money than they ever expected. Do you remember anything in particular from your early days on eBay that went for more than you thought it would?

Roberts: Back then we basically bought collections for a few bucks per piece. Occasionally things would go for $100 or $200, which was a lot of money for us at the time.

In particular, I remember that we got a Peyton Manning autograph for just a few bucks and it ended up selling for $250, which was fantastic. You get those little surprises now and then that kind of keep you going.

Joyner: I understand you initially put all of your profits back into the business in order to grow it, instead of taking cash out from day one.

Roberts: Exactly. For the first two or three years we would occasionally draw a little here and there to pay bills and such. But the money really pretty much went back into the business.

Power**Pointer**

Instead of drawing out income from your business, especially at the start, reinvest it so your company can grow even bigger.

Joyner: Looking back, how did that strategy wind up benefiting you?

Roberts: I don't think we would be as successful as we are now otherwise. In fact, I'm not sure we would still even be in business had I taken some of the income from the start.

I see a lot of merchants doing that. We talk to a lot of people who are interested in starting an eBay business. Most view it as a way to get rich. It's really not. The way to be successful on eBay is to grow it slowly and not think you are going to make that kind of money from it right away. Be patient and let it flourish and grow slowly.

Power**Pointer**

Don't expect to get rich quick. Be patient and let your eBay business grow slowly.

Joyner: Do you still buy collections outright, or do you take items on consignment? What is your business model?

Roberts: We really do both. We buy a lot of collections. We also consign a lot of them.

We basically try to get the person with the collection to consign with us first, assuming they are interested in going that route. Some people just want the money now and aren't interested in consignment. In such cases, we'll make an offer and buy it if it's the right fit. Consignment is best for us because it doesn't require a big up-front initial investment.

Power**Pointer**

The advantage of selling items on consignment is that it doesn't require a huge initial investment in order to obtain inventory.

Joyner: Do you sell exclusively on eBay?

Roberts: Right now almost 100 percent of our business is done on eBay. We have a web site, which we hope to move merchandise on going forward so we can be a little bit less eBay dependent. We'd at least like to have some other revenue streams.

Joyner: Do you find that eBay is still the best place to get customers in your category?

Roberts: As far as customer acquisition is concerned, you can't beat eBay. We have customers from all over the world. Probably about 25 percent of our items go overseas. We ship a lot to the United Kingdom, Germany, Japan, and Australia. EBay provides access to international clientele that you couldn't get anywhere else.

PowerPointer

EBay gives you access to an international audience, unlike any other site of its kind.

Joyner: Are there some types of items in the autograph category that sell better? Can you give me some examples?

Roberts: For us, really, the best is anything vintage. That's from the 1960s or earlier. The reason is that there are not nearly as many forgeries from that era as with the more current celebrities. I would estimate that nine out of ten current autograph auctions being conducted on eBay are forgeries. It's pretty tough to compete in the market to sell authentic autographs under those conditions. We therefore really focus more on the vintage stuff, from the 1800s up to the 1960s.

Joyner: Because there is so much fraud and given the high number of autograph forgeries, how do you protect yourselves? And how do you present your auctions as legitimate?

Roberts: Early on we went through a three-year program with the Universal Autograph Collectors Club (UACC). They are the world's oldest and largest autograph association.

The organization allows dealers to enter a three-year program where your inventory is vetted and your listings are watched to make sure you are selling authentic merchandise. After this period you become what's called a registered dealer. There are only about 200 registered dealers worldwide. That adds an extra layer of accountability for us and makes customers feel much more secure that they are buying something that is legit.

We are also bonded by BuySafe. That's been a huge benefit for us, and one that a lot of customers have commented on. They appreciate having their items bonded. They realize that if we were selling nonlegit items we probably wouldn't go through that process.

Power**Pointer**

Getting bonded is one way to increase confidence among potential buyers.

Joyner: Have you ever listed an autographed item that you thought was legitimate and later found out it wasn't?

Roberts: Absolutely. It happens to every autograph dealer out there. It doesn't matter how good you are; you're going to make mistakes every now and then. I would say it happens maybe a couple of times a year. We immediately offer a full refund in such cases.

Joyner: What happens if it comes to your attention before the sale closes?

Roberts: If something is brought to our attention before it closes we'll cancel all the bids, shut the auction down, and let the customers know why.

Joyner: Do you think there will be a market for items autographed by celebrities today 20 to 30 years from now?

Roberts: That's a good question. I'm kind of skeptical that there will be. The main reason goes back to the forgery problem. I'm a little bit skeptical that celebrities who are popular right now will have much of a marketplace.

Joyner: What sells better for you: autographed sports cards, photographs, or items like signed baseballs?

Roberts: It really varies. As I mentioned, anything vintage definitely does best. Newer stuff is a little harder to sell for a high price, because of the forgery problem.

Anything that is unique, and visibly out of the ordinary, sells well. If you're looking for a Mel Gibson autograph on eBay, you're going to find 100 or 200 of them. But if you have something unique that no one else is selling, those are the items that definitely bring in the most money.

Power**Pointer**

Unique items that are otherwise hard to find on eBay bring in the most money.

Joyner: Of the thousands of items you've sold on eBay, are there any that really stand out?

Roberts: Yes, we sold a Ty Cobb autographed baseball a couple of years ago that went for a couple of thousand dollars. That's a pretty unique item that you don't see on eBay very often.

We had a Beatles autographed magazine that was signed by all the Beatles that went for a several thousand dollars a few years ago. Those kinds of items definitely stand out.

We had an old autograph album that a little girl in the 1930s put together. It was autographed by Franklin Roosevelt, Herbert Hoover, and a lot of very famous people of the day. That went for a couple of thousand dollars.

Joyner: Was the little girl's autograph album personalized, and does that help or hurt the value if it's signed "To Molly," for instance?

Roberts: Again, that varies a lot. For the vintage stuff, it actually doesn't hurt at all. It's nice to have that provenance and people enjoy having a little story behind it. For more modern items, it definitely hurts the value to be personalized.

Joyner: Are there any autographs that you have that you wouldn't let go of? Do you have a wall of fame in your own office or your home?

Roberts: When we started the business, I was also a collector. I found that it was kind of hindering what we were trying to do because there were items that would come through that I would want to keep for my own collection. So, I stopped collecting altogether. Now it's merely a business for us.

Joyner: Everything you sell is unique, usually one of a kind. With 2,000 auctions going at any one time, how do you manage all of that volume?

Power**Pointer**

The key to scaling your business is having an effective automated auction management program.

Roberts: Pretty early on when we decided to scale up our business, we knew it was going to be important to find the right auction management company. So we went out and tried them all out. Most will give you 30 days free. We tested them all, and the one that we found worked the best for us is called AuctionHelper.

The reason it works so well for us is the listing function is all on the same page. Say we have 200 autographed photos to list. All we have to do is change the title and photo on it. We can probably list three or four per minute that way, just by changing a couple of things. We don't have to alter the entire description.

We try to list similar items like that. It cuts our listing time down tremendously.

AuctionHelper offers a very dynamic postauction management program, too. So we really don't have to do much hands-on work anymore. It's pretty much all automated. It's just a matter of scanning the items to get them listed.

Joyner: Are you mostly scanning items rather than photographing them?

Roberts: Probably about 90 percent are scanned.

Joyner: Is that because you get a better depiction of the autographed item than you would with a photograph?

Roberts: Correct, and the items are small enough that it makes more sense to do that, at least for the most part.

Joyner: For my previous book, *The eBay Millionaire*, I interviewed someone who sold vintage movie posters. He had a similar strategy. On one day, he might list only movie posters of a certain size. The next day, he'd list still photographs from movies. He said that helped on the shipping end, too, because the auctions of like items would end at the same time. Do you find this is beneficial for you, too?

Roberts: It definitely makes it easier for our guy in shipping. He can pull a stack of envelopes all the same size and start stuffing those with baseball cards or autographed photographs. Since they are all the same size, it requires a lot less packaging time.

PowerPointer

Consider listing all like items at the same time. That way, the auctions end in sync and you can concentrate on stuffing packages of the same size and specifications, making your shipping operation more efficient.

Joyner: Do you insure every item that ships out of your warehouse?

Roberts: No. In fact, we only insure an item if the costumer requests it, or if it's a pretty expensive item, we'll go ahead and insure it. But most of our items go for a fairly low dollar amount, so we can absorb an occasional lost item. Most of our items sell for under $20. We just sell in large volumes.

Joyner: What's your pricing strategy?

Roberts: Basically it's buy low, sell high. Because we buy large collections or in bulk, we are able to profit even if items sell for only a couple of dollars apiece. If we can turn them around for $5 to $10, we're still making a pretty good profit on each item.

Joyner: Would you list an autographed item for a starting bid of 99 cents?

Roberts: Our main strategy is to price things at 99 cents. Our consigners aren't usually too hip with that because of the risk of losing money. But we do it for our own items. Because we have a pretty good costumer base and reputation, we're usually able to get at least market value and usually much more for items by pricing items this way. It also helps keep our eBay fees low.

Power**Pointer**

A good strategy for moving merchandise is to start auctions at 99 cents. This low starting price point will also save you money in listing costs.

Joyner: When you have consigners who are hesitant to embrace that pricing strategy, what can you say to get them to try it out?

Roberts: That's a good question, and a dilemma we just ran into today. We've got one very large consigner who doesn't like that strategy. He wants to list everything with a high starting bid. As a result, his sell-through rate is very low. What we've done is we've shown him several examples of what happens when you open the bidding low rather than high. (You usually wind up selling the item, and for a fair price.)

We had a consigner recently who had a bunch of old vintage signed baseball cards. He had one in particular, a Sandy Koufax signed rookie card, that he was convinced needed to start at a high price. While he allowed us to list everything else low and let it ride, he was attached to the Koufax card and wanted us to put a $650 minimum bid on it. We listed it two or three times, but it didn't get any bites. I finally convinced him to just let me list it at 99 cents, and it ended up going for $750.

I showed this other hesitant consigner some of those kinds of examples. I still haven't convinced him yet to let me list his items for 99 cents, but I'm working on it.

Joyner: Who are your customers and how do they find you?

Roberts: We actually have a lot of repeat business. In fact, we really want to find more new buyers. The same people buy our stuff over and over again, which isn't a bad problem to have.

We're in kind of a unique position, in that we brought a lot of existing customers with us to eBay. We also have a lot of dealers who buy from us on a regular basis.

As far as repeat customers are concerned, our feedback score is high and we have a lot of people who keep coming back to buy multiple items from us.

Joyner: What can you do to bring in new buyers?

Roberts: For one thing, we have our web site, which is basically informational and directs people to our eBay auctions.

To be honest, I think eBay itself has done a really poor job of attracting new buyers. I just saw a graph today showing that the number of new eBay users who have bought items over the past year has pretty much plateaued.

I think making the marketplace safer would help, so we try to stress that a lot in our auctions. We're a safe place to buy from. If something goes wrong with the transaction, it gets fixed promptly. I think customer security is a huge factor when it comes to bringing in new buyers and keeping repeat buyers.

Joyner: In addition to getting bonded by BuySafe and going through a process like the UACC certification, what are some other things that you or any seller can do to convey that you're a safe merchant to buy from?

Roberts: I think keeping your feedback high, for one thing, is important. I also buy off of eBay a lot, and am extremely wary of anyone with a feedback rating below 99 percent.

I think how you react to customers who leave you less than positive feedback is huge, as well. That's something I look at as a buyer. If something goes wrong with a transaction, I want the seller to make it right. Oftentimes you'll see a seller get negative feedback and then leave a sarcastic comment for the buyer. As a customer, I try to stay away from sellers like that. Maintaining the highest level of professionalism that you can is very important.

Power**Pointer**

If a customer leaves negative feedback about your company, be sure to respond appropriately. Be courteous and understanding, not negative and sarcastic.

Joyner: So it doesn't help your business at all to get into virtual shouting matches with your customers by posting retaliatory negative feedback for them?

Roberts: Not at all. I don't see any benefit in that.

Joyner: Do you sell exclusively through auctions on eBay, or do you ever list items through an eBay store?

Roberts: I do put some things in eBay stores, but those are mostly consignment items. I mentioned the consigner we've got who likes to start things high. If his items don't sell at auction, we put them in the store.

Joyner: So, I'm only going to find higher-priced items in your eBay store?

Roberts: Right.

Joyner: Are there certain listing upgrades that you use regularly that you would recommend?

Roberts: One of the few listing upgrades we use is the gallery, and we only use that on a certain percentage of our items. When we sell auto-graphed photos, we find it's really necessary to have a gallery image. If we're selling an autographed letter or three-by-five cards, it's not that helpful. We will use a gallery image on things like autographed balls and jerseys.

Otherwise, we don't usually use very many listing upgrades. Every once in a while we'll feature an item, but that's pretty rare.

Joyner: Can you give me an example of something you might have featured?

Roberts: For instance, if we're selling a collection all in one lot, we'll often feature it.

We've actually fooled around with this to see what, if any, differ-ence featuring made. We found that it really doesn't make any differ-ence at all. In fact, it barely makes up the $19.95 featured listing fee for us.

Joyner: When you're listing an item for sale on eBay, do you have a tar-get insertion fee?

Roberts: We try to keep our listing fees as low as possible. Basically our goal is to keep the listing fees under 10 percent of revenues.

Joyner: When dealing with consigners who don't take your advice about setting low opening bids for their auctions, are they responsible for paying the additional listing or insertion fees?

Roberts: No, but usually we'll take a larger commission in such cases. Our commissions are generally negotiated.

Joyner: Why do you have negotiated commissions rather than a flat percentage, which is how a lot of people selling on commission oper-ate?

Roberts: To be honest, we do have a flat rate. Our flat rate is 35 percent, and we negotiate it down from there as necessary. The reason we do that is because consigners feel like they are getting a bargain this way.

Though our flat fee is generally 35 percent, we can sometimes go down to 30 percent or 28 percent. It just gives us a little flexibility, depending on the size and amount of the collection. We'll consign anything from $1,000 to $25,000 to upwards of $1 million. With such a range in value, you need the ability to be flexible with fees.

Joyner: Is there a point where a collection is too small for you to bother with? Is $1,000 your threshold?

Roberts: Generally, yes. And the smaller the collection, the higher the commission we charge.

Joyner: What is the most time-intensive part of what you do, and what do you wish you could streamline more?

Roberts: By far the most time-intensive part for us is scanning in each piece. Because we sell autographs, even if we have multiples of the same items, it's really not ethical for us to make one scan and use it for each item. So we have to scan each piece individually, which is pretty time-consuming.

Joyner: How long does it take to scan a single item?

Roberts: A few seconds, but we try to list 300 or 400 items a day. So, you're talking about pretty much half a day to scan items in and the other half to list them.

Joyner: Have you ever shopped around for a faster scanner that can handle more volume?

Roberts: We bought a very cheap scanner early on in our business and found that it's worked the best for us. I keep shopping on eBay for these old scanners, rather than going for the new ones. I have bought about a half dozen of them now.

We've bought some newer ones and found they were actually slower because the software that they use required more steps. We purchased some brand-spanking-new scanners a few months ago, and it probably increased our scanning time three- or fourfold. So, we went back to the old standby scanners that we started with.

We use a very basic scanner with basic software that allows us to go through the process in the fewest steps possible.

Joyner: And what's the name and model number of that trusty scanner?

Roberts: It's just an old HP Scanjet 2200.

Joyner: Do you try to post auctions and/or end your auctions at certain times?

Roberts: Everything is listed between 7 P.M. and 8:30 P.M. Pacific time.

Joyner: And why is that?

Roberts: Those are the times that we've found work the best for us. People are done with supper, everyone's home from work about that time, and it's when they are on the Internet cruising around and shopping.

We've experimented with different times, and we've found that if we go much earlier or later than that, our average selling prices drop significantly. We list pretty much every day, Sunday through Friday. We don't do any Saturday listings. Again, we experimented with those, and Saturday listings were just a disaster for us.

PowerPointer

A good time to list items is between 7 P.M. and 8:30 P.M., Sunday through Friday.

Joyner: I guess people are doing other things on Saturday nights than going on eBay.

Roberts: Exactly.

Joyner: People used to say that Sunday was a great day to have auctions end on eBay. Do you find that sales spike on any other day?

Roberts: Sunday is definitely our best day. We try to keep our most expensive items ending on Sunday.

Power**Pointer**

Sundays are great days for ending auctions.

Joyner: About a quarter of your business is with international customers. Do you find that selling internationally is more challenging than selling domestically? Do you have to be more cognizant of fraud with international buyers?

Roberts: The interesting thing for us is we've found it to be just the opposite. International buyers tend to pay more for the items that they win. We've had almost no problem with fraud from the international buyers. Most of our problems with fraud or fraudulent buyers come from the United States.

Joyner: Why do international customers pay more? Is it simply because your type of merchandise isn't as widely available in their home countries?

Roberts: Yes, and you've got exchange rates and all those things to play into it. We've wondered about the reason for a long time and I don't know that we've come up with a definitive answer, but international customers do pay significantly more.

Power**Pointer**

All other things being equal, international customers will pay more for merchandise than shoppers based in the United States.

Joyner: Well, that's good to hear. International sales are an untapped market for a lot of eBay sellers.

Roberts: That's something I've never really understood.

Joyner: Was there a point where you just made a decision to sell internationally? Or have you always accepted bids from people in other countries?

Roberts: To tell you the truth, when we started selling we were a bit naive about who would be buying. Right off the bat we had quite a few international customers, many of them dealers. We had such good experiences that we never really considered not selling overseas.

Joyner: Are you responsible for dealing with customs and brokerage issues on international orders?

Roberts: Because most of our items are small and can go in an envelope, we don't even have to go through customs issues. We have shipped some autographed guitars and the like overseas, and admittedly that can be a bit challenging. We're fairly fortunate in that we live in a very small town, so we have a good rapport with our postmistress and she helps us out a lot.

Joyner: Given that you live in a small place like that, how do you find merchandise to sell, not to mention consigners?

Roberts: Because we are a large seller on eBay with a good reputation, people generally come to us with inventory.

Joyner: Do you have to travel a lot or go to trade shows in order to find items to sell?

Roberts: No. As a matter of fact, we do very little traveling.

Joyner: So you truly are an Internet-based business from every aspect?

Roberts: From every standpoint, yes.

Joyner: Is the Internet the best place to buy collectibles, or at least the cheapest?

Roberts: If you are buying from us as opposed to from a dealer at a trade show, you'll probably get the item for significantly less. The guys at trade shows are buying wholesale, and we're buying way below wholesale. We're able to charge significantly less for items and still make a good profit. Basically we're selling at market value or a little bit above. The dealers sell at retail or book value. They're going to sell much less than us, but for a much higher price.

Joyner: Does an item's book value hinder you when you're negotiating to buy a collection from one of your suppliers?

Roberts: Yes. They expect to get close to that price, and it's just not realistic. The book values are usually written by dealers with a vested interest in keeping that value up. Book values are so out of the realm of reality when it comes to the online market value.

Power**Pointer**

So-called book values often have little relevancy when it comes to selling in the online world.

Joyner: Do you anticipate that as the online trade of collectibles grows, the whole notion of book value will change?

Roberts: That's an interesting point. I think the market has already changed significantly, yet book values haven't really dropped. Whether they ever will or not, that's a tough question. There's an interest in keeping the book value as high as possible.

Joyner: On eBay, and the Internet in general, it's important for people to realize that something is only worth what someone else is willing to pay for it.

Roberts: You can put a high price on an item, but it will probably sit there in your eBay store for months and months. Maybe eventually the right buyer will come along and snag it. But in the meantime you'll waste all that revenue that could have been generated for many months. For us, it's all about turning things over quickly. That's how we generate maximum revenue. Even if we lose a little bit of money on some items, for us turning items over quickly and being able to reinvest our money in new merchandise is very important.

Joyner: How often are you willing to relist an item?

Roberts: For our consigners, we'll relist it one time. For our own items, we usually don't relist at all.

Joyner: What will you do with those items instead?

Roberts: We throw them in a big lot with similar items and sell them together. For instance, we might auction off a lot of 100 signed photos or 500 signed baseball cards. We'll start the bidding at 99 cents and let it go.

Joyner: What is the best bit of advice you've learned as an eBay seller? What advice would you offer to someone just starting out?

Roberts: Again, I would emphasize that this is a long-term business. Have patience. Don't expect to generate a lot of income right away. Reinvest the money you make into buying more inventory. Slowly build your business, learn the ropes, and cultivate a customer base that will continually come back to your auctions.

Also understand the old saying, "Time is money." This is especially true on eBay. The more time you put into each item that you're listing, the more it's going to cost you. So just reducing the amount of time for each task is extremely important.

PowerPointer

On eBay, time is money. Therefore, reduce the amount of time you spend on each task in order to be more efficient and profitable.

Joyner: That makes perfect sense. Have you ever calculated what you earn per hour?

Roberts: Yeah, we do pretty well. I earn significantly more than I did as a teacher, almost twice as much.

It's interesting how many eBay sellers fail to take into account how much their time is worth when calculating profitability. In other words, if you toil for 10 hours just to make a $50 profit, you're probably better off just keeping your day job, which by law must pay more than $5 an hour. Roberts says even many big sellers make the mistake of looking at cash flow instead of profitability. That can be a fatal error because if one incident slows your cash flow down, you can quickly be run out of business.

Therefore, be sure to stay on top of the bottom line, and always have an understanding of what it really costs to keep your operation running. If the numbers don't add up, you'll need to find a more efficient way of doing business, using the advice and strategies in this book, in order to stay afloat.

2

Adam Hersh

Adam Hersh Auctions

Adam Hersh was chasing a hot stock tip the first time he began perusing eBay. It was 1998. EBay was still a relatively new dot-com and Hersh was a student at Northeastern University in Boston. Although he kept hearing people talk about the web site and eBay's incredible stock price, Hersh didn't know much else about the California-based company.

When he pointed his Web browser to eBay one day, Hersh was amazed by what he found. There were pages and pages of advertisements for used items. And people were buying this stuff for good money, bidding just as fervently as they would at a country auction.

In a flash of inspiration, Hersh decided to try his hand at selling on the web site, too. He literally picked something up off his floor and posted it for auction. The rest, as they say, is history.

Hersh claims he can't even remember the first item he sold, but he does recall that the bids started rolling in quickly. Within a week someone from somewhere across the country had bought and paid for the item.

From there, eBay became an addiction for Hersh. He cleaned out his apartment and sold everything he could get his hands on. In between college classes, he logged more and more time on the auction site.

"Next thing I knew, my whole apartment was empty," he says.

By that time, Hersh started thinking that eBay could be a nice little sideline business—and a good way to earn some fun money—if only he could find a steady source of inventory. Just as he was running out of his own stuff to sell, friends who had heard he was unloading items on eBay and earning cash doing it began asking him to sell for them.

Hersh agreed to help his friends out. Before long, was so inundated with merchandise from others, he forgot about his idea to scout for new inventory of his own. That's when some guy Hersh didn't even know called out of the blue and asked if he could help sell a set of car rims for him on eBay.

In that moment, Hersh had found his niche as one of eBay's first trading assistants, though at the time there wasn't even a name for what he did. Though he'd been selling for free as a favor for friends, the freebies were now over. Hersh agreed to sell the stranger's rims for a cut of the profit, and a new business was born.

Hersh went on to help pioneer eBay's trading assistant program. Now, there are countless others who earn incomes as eBay trading assistants. Yet, many eBay users remain unfamiliar with what these entrepreneurs do.

Simply put, trading assistants sell items for others on eBay. They are experienced eBay sellers, with a feedback score of at least 100 and at least a 97 percent positive rating.

These eBayers work a lot like consignment stores. People bring their unwanted merchandise to the assistants, with the understanding that if the item sells, the trading assistant will take a percentage of the profit.

After graduating from college, Hersh decided to make eBay his full-time career. Hersh has been an active member of the Professional eBay Sellers Alliance (PeSA) for almost a decade and is one of eBay's best-known personalities. He has conducted millions of auctions on the site. In fact, every month he posts thousands of items up for sale under his user ID, adamhersh. His monthly sales fluctuate between the Platinum and Titanium PowerSeller levels, depending on the value of the merchandise sold.

Hersh mostly sells posters and art prints, which are consigned to him by a poster wholesaler. But he also auctions off high-ticket merchandise, including designer clothing, paintings, electronics, and jewelry belonging to other people.

Hersh doesn't do it alone. He has graduated to the next level of trading assistants. He's now an auction broker with a network of nearly 200 trading assistants working under him. As one of eBay's best-known trading assistants, Hersh fields about 20 calls a day from companies and individuals wanting to sell goods on eBay. He cherry-picks the best ones, choosing to accept merchandise only from those individuals with very valuable items or from companies capable of providing him with a large volume of inventory. He farms out the rest to his network, charging a commission for the lead.

Hersh talks with us in the following interview about how he built a successful eBay business as a trading assistant without investing a penny of his own money to buy inventory. He provides the lowdown on how eBay's trading assistant program works, and offers some unique tips for finding consignment merchandise to sell in the online marketplace. He also shares some marketing secrets that can help you earn higher revenues and profits.

Joyner: Your company is now headquartered in New York. But why did you choose Las Vegas as your initial base of operations?

Hersh: I decided to move to the city where I felt the most people would be looking for fast cash—Las Vegas. Where else in the country could I go to find people who were almost begging me to sell their items?

Joyner: What is the benefit of being a trading assistant on eBay?

Hersh: It's a way you can start an eBay business with almost no initial cost. If you get lucky enough to hook up with a company or great individual with a collection of items, you can start your eBay career with no money and just take a little portion off someone else's inventory. It's really a way to get unlimited inventory.

PowerPointer

One way to get started selling on eBay, without investing any money in inventory, is by becoming a trading assistant.

Joyner: Were you surprised, at least initially, that so many people were interested in using trading assistants, given how easy it is to post items up for sale on eBay on your own?

Hersh: There are always going to be people who either don't want to deal with the hassle or are just completely afraid of the Internet, eBay, and computers in general. EBay realized that people were already selling for others and they formalized the trading assistant program. Trading assistants are normally really good sellers. That benefits eBay, which gets a bigger commission from the sale.

Joyner: Once you decided eBay was going to be your business, you came up with an interesting technique for finding merchandise to sell. Could you talk about that?

Hersh: In the very beginning, I was actually hiring people to cold-call individuals who had placed items for sale in classified ads. They would say, "I see you're selling your item. Would you mind if we did it for you on eBay? We can get a better price."

Joyner: And that worked?

Hersh: It did. For a year in college, I used to sell real estate, and that's how I was taught to find new clients who were trying to sell their homes. It's the same concept.

It's not that hard to sell your own home, but a real estate agent will deal with the whole hassle of it. People love that. They're happy to pay you a small percentage to deal with the whole mess.

I was surprised at the amazing response I received as a trading assistant, though I was pretty confident at the start there were people willing to let me sell for them on eBay.

Even after our fee is taken, the client is normally just happy that they didn't have to deal with the hassle on their own.

Joyner: How did you make the leap from trading assistant to auction broker?

Hersh: My eBay business was growing fast, and the calls kept coming in. It was just too much for me to handle—not only in terms of the amount of work, but also in the scope of knowledge. People were calling with antique furniture and artwork and jewelry—things I didn't know about. But I didn't want to turn them away. I wanted to get them taken care of, so I ended up going back into the directory of eBay trading assistants and asking if they'd be willing to take clients from me that I couldn't handle in return for a little percentage of their percentage.

Joyner: When you send leads to other trading assistants, you do your best to find someone who has some expertise and knowledge of the particular product the consigner wants to sell. Why is that important?

Hersh: Half the point of using a trading assistant is that I'm taking the hassle away from you, but the other half is I'm theoretically getting you the best possible price.

I know eBay back and front, and I know marketing tricks and techniques. But if I don't know the type of item, then I can't really maximize the profit. Now I have experts I can rely on for just about anything that comes in.

Power**Pointer**

It's essential to have a strong knowledge of the products you sell in order to evaluate and price them correctly.

Joyner: As a big-time eBay seller, how do you decide whether to take someone's consignment? Are you as interested in buying from individuals as you once were? Or are you looking for consigners who can provide you with a steady stream of merchandise?

Hersh: Smaller consignment accounts aren't really worth it for us, especially if they're one-time items. But if it's a business with small-priced items, there are definitely ways of doing it.

I'm working with two really large companies that each have small-priced items, but we're relying on the volume to produce the income. So, it's just as good as a company that sells 10 really big items weekly.

Joyner: What are some of the mistakes that you see eBay sellers making?

Hersh: Sellers fail to prepare themselves to handle a huge volume of business. The amazing thing about eBay and the Internet is that they are comprised of just a bunch of computers connected with each other. That way, everything can be automated.

Right now, I have thousands of auctions running and not really that many people are managing them because of the automation I've got in place and the auction management software I'm using.

There's always a tool and/or technique that can help you streamline your eBay business. A lot of people don't want to make that step. They feel overwhelmed. They think it's too much for them.

People sometimes say to me, "I like handling everything with a pen and paper, and I like feeling as if I have a grasp on everything." Unless you're willing to just go for it, to take a step forward and hire an auction management company or download one of the listing tools available on eBay, you can never really handle the volume of a top seller.

When it comes to volume, that's just a huge technique: Don't be afraid to outsource to find appropriate listing tools. You can even outsource shipping.

Power**Pointer**

Automate and outsource as many functions as possible. You'll be surprised by how much volume you may need to handle.

Joyner: In your case, you use Marketworks auction management software, correct?

Hersh: Yes.

Joyner: You're really involved in networking on eBay, both through PeSA and by other means. What other tools do you use to learn about what's going on with eBay?

Hersh: I read the "Announcements" message board in eBay's Community section every day. It's the best way to find out anything that eBay has cooking. I always try to think of how I can use the features discussed there right away.

Power**Pointer**

Read the "Announcements" message board in eBay's Community section each day to get the latest on what's happening throughout the site.

Joyner: As an introduction for readers who aren't familiar with it, the Announcements board is updated daily to inform users of the latest changes to eBay. Essentially, it's a place where buyers and sellers can find out about the newest tricks and tools of eBay. The board lists promotions, free listing days, new features on the web site, and other news.

What were some of the mistakes that you made early on in your eBay career?

Hersh: If you put this in the book, it would be hilarious because my friend won't let me live it down. I sold his Rollerblades, and I messed up. I'm pretty sure I misspelled the title, which usually results in no people finding the item. If you misspell something, you limit your audience to one or two people.

Power**Pointer**

Check spelling carefully when writing up your listing. If you misspell a name, no one will be able to find your item.

The skates ended up going for $1. Years later, now that I'm touring around and speaking about how to sell online, he'll sometimes yell at me, "You're not an eBay expert. You sold my Rollerblades for $1!"

My one buying technique to find a great deal on eBay is to purposefully misspell the word when I search. I bought some Britney Spears concert tickets for my girlfriend, and I misspelled Britney Spears on purpose and found a pair of tickets really cheap. So, it works well for buyers, but not sellers.

Joyner: You list some items on eBay for 99 cents and others for $9.99 or $19.99. What's the benefit in starting the bidding low, say 99 cents?

Hersh: EBay has proven time and time again that when you list an item at $1 or less, most of the time you get a higher price than if you had started the bidding at a higher price.

There are a lot of reasons for that. One, people sort by price very often, usually beginning with the lowest, so you get that bid right away.

Two, psychologically when someone sees two auctions and one has a bid and one doesn't, people like to bid on the one that already has bids. Auctions with bids get more bids because they look more appealing.

Number three, let's say that you start this thing at $20, but I start my same item at one penny. When I'm at $20, I might have three or four people involved already, and you might have your first bidder or nobody. My three or four people keep on getting e-mail letters from eBay that say, "You've been outbid. Would you like to rebid?"

It's funny, but people just get pissed. When they get that outbid e-mail, they go back and they bid more. You just create this momentum when you start an auction lower.

PowerPointer

> By starting bids at a lower price, you will create more interest
> and momentum as buyers compete to bid higher against
> each other.

Joyner: So, you like starting auctions for well below the item's value?

Hersh: Ideally, I would love to start every auction at a penny and just let it ride. Because I'm selling on consignment, it's very hard to convince people to start their auction very low. I have definitely started cars and very expensive items very low and they've gone for a fair price.

For one-of-a-kind items, like a unique piece of art, I would not start it at a penny. But if there's an item that you know there's an eBay market for, I'd be very confident that you could start bidding at a penny or a dollar and you'd get a better price.

Joyner: How do you feel about reserve-price auctions?

Hersh: I don't like reserves. I would rather start the opening price higher than even have a reserve on the auction.

Joyner: Do you think more experienced sellers avoid reserve-price auctions because there's a fee?

Hersh: It's very expensive. Fortunately, if the reserve gets met, eBay actually gives you your money back. But if it doesn't sell, you end up paying a good amount. I would rather start an item really high.

PowerPointer

> It's better to start the bidding at a higher price than to use
> reserves.

Joyner: Do you ever use reserves?

Hersh: Sometimes. Somebody will call me and say, "I have this item that I need sold." I will look up the eBay price, which is really all I care about, and say, "I can sell it for X amount of dollars." And they say, "No, no, no. I need $5,000 more than that. I know what it's worth. I have a price book."

I don't know where these price guides are made, but I say, "Listen, I know how to sell on eBay, and I'm just telling you I can get this X price because I looked at completed auctions and several different web sites." I know what things go for on eBay.

So, I'll say, "Why don't we start it at a penny, and we'll put the reserve price at your ridiculous price?" And what ends up happening is the auction doesn't reach their price, like I knew it wouldn't, but it ends up reaching another price.

Now I get to show them the completed auction and say, "Somebody would have paid $3,500 for it. It's too bad our reserve was $7,000." And they say they would have sold it for $3,500. So, I actually use the reserve in a way most people probably don't, and that is as kind of a convincing tool.

Joyner: The mentality of an amateur eBay seller sounds very much like what happens at a yard sale. You put your price on a piece of junk—say $10—and then someone offers you $5 and you agree to sell it for that, since $5 is what you really expected in the first place.

Hersh: Exactly. Except if you price something at a penny at a garage sale somebody might grab it. The real beauty of eBay is it has millions of registered users all in the same marketplace. All you need are two or three interested people to start a bidding war.

Joyner: How do you make sure that people pay for the items they buy from you? Do you still accept checks and money orders?

Hersh: Absolutely. I'll accept any way that someone is willing to pay because it will only help increase the price for each item.

I've heard that I have a lower nonpaying bidder ratio than many top sellers. I send out a lot of payment reminders and nonpaying bidder warnings. It's all automated. These messages say something to the effect that, "You haven't paid for the item. We're going to file a nonpaying bidder alert tomorrow if we haven't heard from you. And this is what a nonpaying bidder alert can do to your account."

As far as personal checks are concerned, for anything above $5 or $10 we wait for it to clear before the item actually ships.

Power**Pointer**

Be open to accepting all forms of payment. For personal checks, wait for the funds to clear before shipping the item.

Joyner: How important is feedback to buyers and sellers?

Hersh: Feedback is really the foundation of eBay. If you think about it, you're selling to a complete stranger. When I first started selling, I thought it was amazing that I was getting checks in the mail from people in China, Canada, New Mexico, and Kansas, and they didn't even know who I was.

It's come to the point, of course, where now I have one of the top feedback ratings and reputations. People trust me because of the reputation I've established. But at the beginning, it was extremely important to build that feedback because that really is going to be your whole trust level.

Joyner: When I've bought and sold things on eBay, I've found that feedback is very reciprocal. If you leave me good feedback, I'll leave you feedback. But if you don't bother to leave me any feedback, I'm not going to bother to leave you any. Do you find that's the case?

Hersh: It is very reciprocal. Very often, it's the seller's responsibility to leave feedback as soon as he receives payment, and then the buyer will leave feedback as soon as they receive the item.

Power**Pointer**

Feedback is reciprocal. Leave feedback as soon as you receive payment for an item.

Joyner: Do you ever leave negative feedback?

Hersh: Occasionally. But I feel it's more important to let eBay know if somebody hasn't paid for an item. If you file a nonpaying bidder alert, eBay takes that very seriously and eventually gives the bidder a warning and possibly suspends them.

The feedback loop is so important because, as you know by now, good feedback gives buyers the confidence to do business with you. As illustrated by Hersh's experience, treating buyers right often results in more positive treatment for you. After all, good customer service matters just as much in the online world as it does in any other forum.

3

David Yaskulka
Blueberry Boutique

David Yaskulka was working as the chief marketing officer for a national nonprofit organization when his wife, Debbie, came up with an idea that would allow her to earn some extra money while staying at home with their twin sons. Eventually, their professional pursuits would become inextricably intertwined, creating a new model for doing business on eBay.

Debbie Yaskulka's initial business plan wasn't that ambitious. Her goal was to work about 10 hours a week selling merchandise on eBay. She had very reasonable financial expectations: to clear just $150 a week, or about $7,800 a year. But things didn't quite happen that way.

When their venture was new, the Yaskulkas stumbled onto another eBay merchant who was offering a wholesale lot of men's designer neckties. They bought the ties at a good price and sold them individually for a profit on eBay. That one deal officially launched the Yaskulkas into business and paved the way for their company, Blueberry Boutique, which has now become the leading auction seller of shirts and ties worldwide with outlets and/or a presence on eBay, Amazon, Overstock, Yahoo! Shopping, Shopzilla, Froogle, Shopping.com, Smarter.com, and their own web site, www.blueberryboutique.net.

Within six months, David left his job with the nonprofit to become chief executive officer of Blueberry Boutique, which sells under the eBay user ID blueberryboutique.

In the summer of 2006, Harris Michael Jewelry, an online retailer of fine jewelry, acquired Blueberry Boutique. David was named president of the combined company and charged with growing the two brands both on eBay and beyond. Debbie, free to return to work now that the children are in school, returned to her earlier career as a special education teacher.

Blueberry Boutique's success story would read like any other PowerSeller's but for one important twist. By drawing on David's nonprofit experience, the Yaskulkas have successfully been able to leverage cause marketing to help the charities they support, while also improving the bottom line for their business. About half of Blueberry Boutique's (and now Harris Michael's) eBay auctions are linked to charities. In these auctions, 10 percent or more of the proceeds are earmarked for such organizations as the National Center for Missing and Exploited Children, the Disabled Online Users Association, and the effort to help victims of Hurricane Katrina.

Through its Giving Works program, eBay allows merchants to host charitable auctions and donate anywhere from 10 percent to 90 percent of the sale price to a worthy cause. Sellers incur no additional fees for running charity auctions, although they must agree to a minimum donation of $5. According to David Yaskulka, who has also helped other eBay PowerSellers with charitable auctions and cause marketing campaigns, such auctions generally result in higher selling prices and conversion rates, a boon to both the charity and the online merchant.

In the following pages, David Yaskulka talks about his company's own experiences with cause-related online marketing. He explains in detail how the eBay Giving Works program functions and shares some hard-earned best practices for conducting charitable auctions. Finally, he offers practical advice and how-to tips to those interested in using charitable auctions to increase their profits and exposure on eBay.

Joyner: Let's start by talking more about the history of your company, and how you came to be in the position you are in today.

Yaskulka: We now have two company histories to talk about. Unlike Blueberry Boutique, which started out as an eBay venture, Harris Michael began as an Internet retailer of fine jewelry and tiptoed, if you will, into the eBay market.

One of the ways it did so was by hiring my Blueberry Consulting firm for a small marketing project. Shortly thereafter I stopped charging Harris for consulting calls because I was learning as much on the calls as they were. We just happened to have knowledge in different areas, which ultimately led to Harris Michael's acquisition of Blueberry Boutique.

Joyner: Blueberry Boutique traces its roots to eBay. The company wouldn't have existed without eBay. What was it about the online auction marketplace that led you to realize this was where you needed to be?

Yaskulka: If you think about our original goal of starting a part-time, very low-intensity business, there really is no place other than eBay where you can do this. The barrier of entry is far lower on eBay than in any other marketplace. I don't even think there's anything at all that comes close.

Power**Pointer**

If you're looking to become an online entrepreneur on just a part-time basis, eBay is arguably the best game in town.

Joyner: Is that because the other online marketplaces can't offer the audience or customer base that eBay does?

Yaskulka: It's really a combination of having access to a large audience of customers without needing to scale any of your operations. In other words, you could find similar or even greater audiences elsewhere outside of eBay, but in order for that to happen you'll need to make some sort of investment.

Joyner: Juxtapose the beginnings of your company with that of Harris Michael, which started out as an e-commerce business and only later began selling on eBay. How did these two companies come together?

Yaskulka: Well, Harris Michael began as a more pure e-commerce company focusing on its own site at www.harrismichaeljewelry.com.

As Blueberry Boutique grew, we realized that one of the major differences between trying to run a small part-time business that can remain profitable week after week and a larger full-time business with employees and a capacity to grow is that the larger one is quite reliant on the supply side. Blueberry never had a competitive advantage on the supply side.

My background is really in marketing, and especially cause-related marketing.

Joyner: And from all reports, you're very good at it.

Yaskulka: But at a certain point, unless you gain significant supply-side advantages, all the great marketing in the world will probably not help you grow any further.

It became clear to me about a year ago that for Blueberry Boutique to continue to flourish, it needed to partner with another company with much greater strength on the supply side.

Power**Pointer**

In order to significantly grow and expand your business, you'll need ongoing access to sufficient inventory at good prices.

Joyner: You're saying that before the acquisition, Blueberry Boutique was not negotiating better deals than your competitors on inventory, or at least not enough for you to gain a competitive advantage?

Yaskulka: That's right.

When I examined different ways in which to leverage Blueberry's greatest strengths in marketing and cause marketing, it was really natural for us to partner with a company with much greater strengths in the supply chain and with their own Web presence—hence, the merger with Harris Michael.

There was a real sort of synergy between these two companies, and we both believe in doing well by doing good.

PowerPointer

Look for synergies with other like business and find ways to effectively work together. Who knows? You might even eventually decide to merge your operations into one such compatible company.

Joyner: "Doing well by doing good." You've quite eloquently and succinctly defined cause marketing, which is where companies align themselves with charities and good causes for their mutual benefit. I certainly want us to talk about your company's involvement in this because you've taken a really unique approach on eBay and frankly in the e-commerce space by embracing cause marketing.

Yaskulka: Here's the problem: If you're a small or medium-sized business, which is almost everyone on eBay, it's very hard to do great cause-related marketing. This is especially true when it comes to the world of e-commerce.

Look at Target, which is a very big company. It partners with the American Red Cross. Macy's, another big retailer, partners with the Make-A-Wish Foundation. That makes perfect sense because their audience is quite wide and they need a big nonprofit brand to partner with.

Let's say I'm a $2 million bricks-and-mortar business on Main Street in Omaha, Nebraska. If I want to build my brand using the same best practices that Macy's and Target are using, instead of partnering with the Red Cross I can partner with the local relief organization, or with a local hospital that has a program like the Make-A-Wish Foundation. It works perfectly because all of my customers are from Omaha and they all know the name of the local hospital or relief organization; that means a lot to them.

But if you're an e-commerce company, your audience and customer base is so widespread. They don't care about what's going on in Omaha; they care about a much wider group of causes.

When Blueberry Boutique contacted the Red Cross right after Hurricane Katrina in hopes of initiating a cause marketing campaign, the Red Cross told us what it would tell everybody: "We require a quarter-million-dollar minimum donation to do a cause marketing program. If you want to donate, that's fine. We'll certainly accept any donation. But if you want your business to benefit, we have to put that through our marketing department and our legal department, and make sure you're not selling anything we don't want sold on our behalf. We need to make sure that you're reliable and that the donation really comes through."

The Red Cross is at the extreme end, but a quarter of a million dollars is the minimum ticket there. Many other top nonprofit brands might have a $100,000 minimum donation, or certainly at least tens of thousands per cause marketing program. Well where does that leave your average e-commerce small or medium-sized business practice? It leaves you behind.

Power**Pointer**

Most large nonprofit organizations have a high barrier you must meet in order to get permission to advertise that you are donating a portion of your sales to the charity. Some even require a minimum commitment, often in the area of tens or hundreds of thousands of dollars.

Joyner: Interesting. So, it's not just as simple as contacting one of these organizations and saying you want to partner up with them? They have stringent requirements for forming such associations. When you heard the minimum required amount from the Red Cross, what was your reaction?

Yaskulka: Certainly there's no opportunity for me there. Fortunately, the Red Cross also told us our other option was to go to eBay and sell through the eBay Giving Works program. This program enables you to partner with any one of 8,000 nonprofit organizations, at least a few hundred of which are top nonprofit brands, and you can use their logos in your auction listings. In turn, these nonprofits will advertise your charitable eBay auctions on their MissionFish home page. (MissionFish provides the technology tools and other infrastructure necessary for eBay merchants to sell items to benefit charity.)

The best thing is there's no campaign minimum and it's a 10 percent donation per listing. EBay is once again providing that small or medium-sized company with an opportunity to do a very big-business type of thing with exceedingly little investment.

Joyner: Was Hurricane Katrina the first time Blueberry Boutique experimented with cause marketing on eBay? Or had your company conducted charitable online auctions before?

Yaskulka: There's a little bit of a curveball to the story. Previously, we were huge believers in cause-related marketing. It just so happens that I have a very strong background in that area, so I was able to find a large national nonprofit willing to form a partnership with me at a much lower minimum donation. They were able to fast-forward it through their legal department.

Joyner: What charity did you support with Blueberry Boutique's initial cause marketing effort?

Yaskulka: The National Center for Missing and Exploited Children. I was able to get to know them through the Professional eBay Sellers

Alliance because we did a charity event for the organization. Officials there recognized us as experts and high-integrity cause marketers.

Joyner: That's why they green-lighted your proposal and allowed Blueberry Boutique to auction off items to benefit the National Center for Missing and Exploited Children?

Yaskulka: Yes, but that would not be an easy path for most eBay sellers. It's not easy to do cause-related marketing outside of the eBay Giving Works program.

Power**Pointer**

> The eBay Giving Works program is a great way for small online businesses to establish a connection and donate a percentage of profits to their favorite charities.

Joyner: What did eBay require you to do to prove that your charitable auction was legitimate?

Yaskulka: I followed eBay's rules and put together a letter from the national nonprofit in my listing saying that we were authorized to sell on its behalf and would donate 10 percent of the proceeds to the organization.

Joyner: But it's clearly easier to sell through the eBay Giving Works program, which is the approach most online auctioneers should take.

Yaskulka: From eBay's perspective, and I support this belief 100 percent, eBay needs to know for sure that if something is purportedly being sold for charity on the site, the money will actually go to the charity. That's the most important thing.

Now how do you do that? It's not easy. It started with the solution of requiring sellers to post a letter from the nonprofit acknowledging that it was familiar with the seller and trusted the seller to give the money. But we know it's pretty easy to fudge such a document.

That's why eBay partnered with MissionFish, which makes sure that the money goes to the charity. From the perspective of marketplace integrity, that infrastructure was necessary.

Joyner: Would you explain how someone goes about selling through the Giving Works program?

Yaskulka: In order to sell through the eBay Giving Works program, you need to register with MissionFish (www.missionfish.org). MissionFish is part of the Points of Light Foundation, one of the largest and most respected volunteer organizations in the country. When you register, you need to put your credit card on file with MissionFish to cover any donations.

Power**Pointer**

To get started with eBay Giving Works, you must first register with MissionFish at www.missionfish.org.

After an auction ends, MissionFish essentially sends the seller an invoice for the donation. But many sellers, including us, are happy to ignore that invoice and know that within about a week or so if we don't pay it, MissionFish just draws it from our credit card. We like that because we prefer not to do any work that we don't have to!

Joyner: So, there's really no additional work required of sellers who decide to donate a portion of their auction sales to charity, other than keeping that money aside and ready to pay off once the credit card bill arrives?

Yaskulka: Exactly.

Joyner: What happens next?

Yaskulka: MissionFish will escrow that donation money for about a month. This allows the seller to complete the sale. If the seller encounters a nonpaying bidder or the item is returned, the seller can request a refund of the donation and MissionFish will, in fact, refund it.

Joyner: Technically, how easy or difficult is it to launch a charitable auction on eBay?

Yaskulka: If you are a professional seller on eBay, you need anything you do on eBay to integrate with your software solution. For a long period of time, eBay Giving Works was not integrated into any of the auction management software solutions. You could launch a charitable auction only through the "Sell Your Item" form on eBay.

Fortunately, that has changed. Now, you can easily launch an eBay Giving Works auction through Turbo Lister, through Selling Manager Pro, and now, most recently, through ChannelAdvisor, which is really a huge step forward.

Joyner: Obviously that will make it easier for other PowerSellers and professional eBayers to become involved in cause marketing.

Often on eBay's home page, bidders will see ads for charitable auctions. Does selling through Giving Works provide online auctioneers with greater exposure? Do charitable auctions get better play and therefore attract more bidder traffic?

Power**Pointer**

Selling through Giving Works gives your site added exposure in a number of ways.

Yaskulka: Absolutely. This happens in a number of different ways. An eBay Giving Works listing gets exposure in areas in which a normal auction item does not.

It's also listed both on the Giving Works page on eBay, which gets a good deal of traffic, and on the MissionFish web site, which also gets a lot of exposure. It's kind of like getting to list in a couple of extra categories without incurring extra listing fees.

Second, eBay is taking specific steps to drive traffic to eBay Giving Works items. At the recent eBay Live! Conference, numerous guest speakers talked about Giving Works and social responsibility.

EBay is starting to see what a valuable program this is, from both a charitable and a business perspective.

EBay is making it easier for people to buy the way they want and for people to sell the way they want. People love supporting causes, and eBay allows small or medium-sized businesses to engage in world-class cause-related marketing in an affordable way.

EBay is now doing home page advertising, e-mail advertising, category page advertising, My eBay page advertising, and other things to drive additional traffic to eBay Giving Works items.

Joyner: Can you talk about the results sellers might expect from Giving Works auctions? How does participation in the program affect the selling price? And how should sellers determine what percentage of each sale they should donate to charity?

Yaskulka: In terms of the impact on the selling price, every seller will have his or her own sort of calculus there. As for how much to donate, I believe from a strategic business perspective there are really just two percentages to choose from: 10 percent, which is the minimum, or 100 percent, which is the max.

A 10 percent donation gets your listing into the eBay Giving Works traffic flow. Whether you choose 10 percent or 100 percent, you get the same amount of additional traffic. You get that special ribbon icon in eBay search results denoting yours is an eBay Giving Works auction. So, for commodity items where the goal is still trying to make money as a salesperson, I recommend a donation of 10 percent.

Power**Pointer**

Unless you're looking to donate all of your proceeds to charity, 10 percent of the total sale price is a good number to target.

However, sometimes there may be items that are high-profile or particularly interesting—the sort of thing that will attract media attention. I recommend for those sorts of items that you donate 100 percent to the charity. From a brand-building and publicity standpoint, you're far better off donating the entire proceeds.

Joyner: Could you provide an example of when you chose to donate 100 percent from an auction to charity versus 10 percent?

Yaskulka: Actually, we are essentially commodity sellers, and always choose to donate 10 percent.

Joyner: As a seller, when you're conducting charitable auctions, how much does that affect your profit margin? Can you expect your selling price to improve when the auction is for charity? In other words, what is the risk or cost to the seller?

Yaskulka: There is a risk, which needs to be managed. But we have found that that risk has rewarded us quite well. As a result, the program has mostly been cost-negative for us. We have found that on eBay you can often run a program like this for almost no money, or even make more money than you otherwise would have because of the auction.

This benefit is realized in one of two ways. For storefront inventory items sold through eBay Giving Works, we have much greater sales velocity. In the case of items sold at a fixed price through our eBay store, it's obviously not that we're achieving higher sales prices. Rather, we're selling more items more quickly, so we can afford to make that 10 percent donation and still make some money. These are incremental sales for us.

If we do a more classic auction, starting at $1 with no reserve, we find that our selling prices go up more than 10 percent because of the charitable component.

Power**Pointer**

Remember, when you promise to donate a certain percentage to charity, you have to live up to your commitment. Therefore, price your products and manage your risks accordingly.

Joyner: Could you hazard a guess as to why that might be?

Yaskulka: It's a whole long list of factors that you can roughly divide into two buckets: one—more traffic; and two—buyer interest in charity items.

What we do know is that, all else being equal, 86 percent of consumers would rather choose a brand that supports a cause they believe in than one that doesn't. And that's a big differential.

PowerPointer

Eighty-six percent of online shoppers would rather buy from a merchant supporting a cause they believe in.

Joyner: Definitely. Clearly, partnering with a charity can be good for business. But I would think it could work the other way, too. I guess you have to be careful about the causes you choose to support because of the message it may send to your customers.

Yaskulka: Absolutely. And I'm happy to talk about how you should choose.

Joyner: Please do, because there are many charities that some people may find innocuous that other consumers wouldn't like. One that stands out and often generates a lot of debate is the Boy Scouts of America because of the organization's antigay stance.

Yaskulka: That's a great example.

It's very strategically important to pick the right nonprofit. As a general rule, you should try to avoid controversy, although sometimes supporting a controversial cause can work to your benefit. If constituents of the Boy Scouts feel under attack, they might go out of their way to buy something from a business supporting the organization. In this case, cause marketing can also become a form of niche marketing, if you will.

Joyner: And if you don't support the organization, you'll likely take your business elsewhere. Given that, how can niche cause marketing work to a seller's advantage?

Yaskulka: Let's say there's some small nonprofit in Omaha that's doing a great job communicating to its constituents about all the eBay merchants selling on its behalf. The organization puts this announcement in its newsletter and on its web site, and talks about it at meetings, even though it's a small nonprofit. If I'm a seller in Omaha, I might decide to support that small local charity, even though it doesn't get nearly as much traffic as the Boys and Girls Clubs of America. The difference is the Boys and Girls Clubs have a lot of merchants selling on their behalf, meaning there's more competition for charitable bidders' dollars.

By supporting a local charity, I can be the big fish in this pond. Even though there are only a few hundred bidders interested in this organization, a few hundred people in Omaha are all shopping with me. That could be a great advantage.

Power**Pointer**

Supporting controversial charities could hurt or help your business. While it may stir the interest of the organization's most ardent fans, it could keep those opposed to the group from buying your products.

Joyner: How much do you have to rely on the charity doing its part in helping to publicize these auctions to its membership or its constituents?

Yaskulka: I think there are thousands of organizations around the country doing vital work. But I always try to think about what will help me donate the most. The way I can donate the most is by supporting nonprofits that also help me generate sales.

We specifically try to choose nonprofits that we think will give us a business advantage by driving additional traffic to our eBay listings. This additional traffic basically comes from three areas: traffic eBay drives, traffic high-profile agencies drive, and traffic we drive.

Joyner: Is it important to time your charitable auctions so they coincide with the charities' own high-profile initiatives? For example, October is National Breast Cancer Awareness Month. Is that a good time to support breast-cancer-related causes?

Yaskulka: Absolutely.

EBay Giving Works and MissionFish have just introduced a new concept, which I think is absolutely fantastic. It's called Spotlight on a Cause. There's a calendar for the year of what causes will be featured when.

In August and September, shoppers are thinking back to school, so the spotlight is on education. In October, just as you would guess, the spotlight is on breast cancer awareness. In November and December, that's holiday time. People are doing holiday shopping, but it's also a time when we want to think about less fortunate children. Not surprisingly, the spotlight is on children who through either childhood diseases or childhood poverty don't have the same advantages as others shopping on eBay. In January people are making New Year's resolutions, so we look at fitness nonprofits.

Merchants can refer to that calendar at different times for cues on when it really will make sense to support different nonprofits.

Yaskulka says that at any one time about half of his listings are linked to one charitable cause or another, meaning that 10 percent of the proceeds go to a designated nonprofit organization. For more on the eBay Giving Works program, visit http://givingworks.ebay.com.

4

Dan Glasure

Dan's Train Depot

Dan Glasure was born to wheel and deal.

As proof, the 32-year-old businessman often relates how he bought a rare Spider-Man comic book for a nickel at a garage sale when he was just eight years old. He resold it later that same day for $100 and agreed to lead the buyer to other comic book bounties in exchange for a finder's fee.

Given that history, it's no surprise that Glasure now makes his living wheeling and dealing, specifically through buying model trains from collectors and reselling them for a profit through his company, Dan's Train Depot. The business operates on eBay, through an e-commerce web site, and from a retail storefront in Ocala, Florida. The company's sales total about $2.5 million annually. The most impressive thing about that revenue figure is that it has remained steady during a period of tremendous change. Specifically, in 2006 Glasure streamlined operations and cut his staffing levels in half, meaning that he's now churning more profit from the same revenue base.

Glasure, who sells under the user ID danstraindepot, got his start on eBay eight years ago, selling the comic books and toy trains he had collected. As his desire for collecting dwindled, Glasure's passion for eBay grew, especially when he saw how much money he could make.

Not long into his new hobby, Glasure spotted an advertisement in the *Thrifty Nickel*, a free trader magazine that he picked up at a local gas station. Another train buff—someone who had obviously spent years and a lot of his discretionary income building his collection—was looking to sell it.

Glasure convinced his father, who had just started a franchise carpet-cleaning business, to underwrite his purchase of the $27,000 collection by taking out a second mortgage on the family home. Buoyed by his earlier online auction successes, Dan felt confident that he could sell the huge train collection on eBay piece by piece at a nice profit.

His dad, who believed in Dan and his idea, leveraged the family home to buy the collection and jump-started yet another family business. Father and son remained partners for three years, until the elder Glasure's death five years ago. Eventually their eBay business became lucrative enough to push them out of the carpet-cleaning business altogether.

Their road to success was paved one purchase at a time, starting with that $27,000 collection. Unlike many collectibles merchants on eBay, Glasure has never believed in selling on consignment—that is, taking a cut in exchange for selling items online for someone else. "I always felt that was kind of the poor man's way out," he says. "Sometimes you've got to spend money to make money." Instead, Glasure prefers to have complete control over his inventory. That's why he and his employees travel the country buying complete train sets and components from other collectors, which they then resell on eBay or one of the company's other outlets.

Until recently, Glasure hasn't taken much profit from Dan's Train Depot. At one point, he personally pocketed less than $50 a week, hardly enough to pay for a week's worth of fast-food meals. Instead, Glasure has funneled most of the cash back into the business in order to build up inventory. He credits this strategy for the company's continued revenue growth and current profitability.

Glasure, whose mentor is a university business professor, believes that to be successful, eBay sellers must treat their operations like a real business. Here he explains how having a business plan, investing in inventory, spending money where it counts, and smart operational planning have helped transform this little hobby into a multimillion-dollar business.

Joyner: Your eBay business was jump-started when you and your dad bought that large train collection and started auctioning off the components online. How successful was that initial venture?

Glasure: We made some money, though I don't think we did as well as we had hoped. But it was certainly an education. We definitely didn't lose money and it was a springboard to what we have now. By the time we bought the next train collection, I had learned a lot. We were then better able to determine what items were worth and I quickly learned that one engine isn't as valuable as another one, along with what a difference the condition of an item makes. If it has a small scratch, does that cut the value in half? In some cases yes, and others no. While you try to learn as much of this stuff as possible in advance, sometimes you can't absorb everything you need to know without actually getting out there and selling—learning on the job, if you will.

Joyner: Did you initially use collectors' books or other tools to estimate the value of the trains you were selling?

Glasure: I looked straight on eBay and searched for what identical and similar completed auctions sold for. Train shows were another way we educated ourselves. We paid attention to what stuff was selling for there. I also had some knowledge because I'd bought little collections and sold them at local hobby stores through ads in the paper and so forth.

PowerPointer

Education and research are your best guides for determining how to price items for sale on eBay.

Joyner: And you also collected trains yourself, right?

Glasure: Oh yes, I was into trains. It was a hobby. Anytime it's your hobby you already have a base of knowledge there that you've gathered by just enjoying the activity. That can help your eBay business. By selling trains, I had a distinct advantage that I wouldn't have had if I had instead chosen to sell something else.

Joyner: After purchasing that first collection, how did eBay morph into a full-time business for you?

Glasure: We put an ad in the local paper indicating that we were looking to buy trains. We found a number of small collections, and then we had a chance to buy some brass locomotives, which is what we kind of specialize in now. We bought six of those, largely just out of gut impulse. We paid around $100 each for them, which we thought was too much. We did very well, though. The next time around, we bought a $45,000 collection full of brass locomotives.

Then we put an ad in a collectors' trade magazine and started going around the country and buying things. We kept reinvesting the money we made back into new collections.

At this point, my dad was still working in the carpet-cleaning business, and I was selling on eBay full-time. I wasn't making money, though—only around $50 a week. Instead, we split the carpet-cleaning money and sank everything we were making off the eBay trains back into the business.

PowerPointer

In order to grow your business, be willing to invest your profits back into it—especially in the beginning.

Joyner: So, it wasn't a very glamorous or lucrative beginning?

Glasure: It took a couple of years before we truly made anything.

Joyner: Did you have to borrow money to get your hands on that $45,000 collection?

Glasure: We did. At one point we were probably a couple hundred thousand dollars in debt. But we always had more inventory than debt, and that's just what it took for us to build this online business. There was some risk involved but it was calculated.

Joyner: Though you're selling unique items, it sounds like you take the approach that many PowerSellers do and prefer to buy inventory in bulk rather than piece by piece. With collectibles, however, I would think it might sometimes be difficult to find large collections. At what point does one amass a huge collection of trains and then decide they're going to sell it?

Glasure: There are generally only a few reasons that entire collections are sold. One, of course, is if the collector dies and it's an estate sale. The other scenario is if they think they're going to die and they don't want to leave everyone with it. Another reason is the collector moves and they've got all this stuff in the basement and can't bring it with them. And sometimes people, even though they had fun with the hobby, are ready to do something else with their lives and will sell out.

Not every deal is that big, either. A lot of our deals are just maybe a few hundred dollars. That was especially true early on.

Joyner: How do you get inventory these days?

Glasure: We advertise in trade magazines. Of course, we have a reputation as a dealer now, which helps. We do buy new products from manufacturers and retailers sometimes, although we still deal heavily with estates and large collections.

We always pay a fair price. We never try to come in as the low bidder. We've never tried to get things as cheap as humanly possible and rip people off. We've tried to be very honest and up-front and tell people that obviously we're going to make a little money on this, but we're still going to pay a fair price. We normally pay about half to 60 percent of what we feel we can sell the inventory for on eBay.

Power**Pointer**

When buying used merchandise to resell, be honest and up-front. That will preserve your reputation and cause others to want to do business with you down the line.

Joyner: You purchase all of your inventory outright, whereas many sellers prefer to deal on consignment. Do you feel that your business is hurt at all because of this?

Glasure: Well, we're still here and a lot of consignment sellers aren't. And we're thriving more than ever.

I don't like consignment because then someone else dictates how we list and sell items, and for how much. I don't want those headaches. I don't like the problems that can ensue.

With consignment, you may take someone's collection, sell 20 percent of it very fast, and make the person extremely happy. But when it comes to the other 80 percent, it moves slowly and you may have to sacrifice it for a lower price. I don't want to have to deal with a collector saying, "I'm not going to take less than this for that, and I don't want you starting the auction at 99 cents."

I like to have the control of my eBay sales. When we get a collection, we know it will even out, in terms of profit. I know there are certain things that we're going to have to sell for half of what they're worth in order to move them, but then we're going to make that money up on the other things.

This is the only way we've been able to keep a flow going. We haven't been encumbered with the problem of dealing with different consigners.

Power**Pointer**

Understand the pros, cons, and limitations of taking
merchandise on consignment versus buying outright.

Joyner: The reason I ask these questions about consignment is because
a lot of people have this notion that selling items for others is a low-
cost way to get started on eBay. And there are certainly some PowerSellers who have built big online businesses by becoming trading
assistants and consigning items for others, including a few in this
book.

Glasure: It can be an easy way to get started, I'll grant you that.

Joyner: How do you price things to sell on eBay? For instance, do you
prefer to open the bidding at 99 cents like some other merchants?

Glasure: We used to always do 99-cent opening bids with everything.
We have changed that in the last few years because the market has
changed. I still never do reserves, but we will do a minimum bid.

Joyner: What has happened to the market that forced you to make that
switch?

Glasure: There has been a flood of items priced at that level, and eBay
has changed, too.

Joyner: You actually have a web site and a retail store. How did you
come to open those channels? As you said earlier, in the beginning you
were selling exclusively on eBay.

Glasure: EBay was a great springboard for us and we would have never
had this business without it. I never could have sold the same amount
of stuff in my little town from a retail storefront.

The retail store came to be because we needed a warehouse. Instead of just warehousing the stuff, we figured we could put it in a
store. There are certain things that sell better in a retail store than online, such as cheap little items that people don't want to pay shipping

for. On the flip side, there are high-ticket items that collectors won't purchase at a physical store, but will buy on eBay.

Our retail store is not nearly as profitable for us as the e-commerce business.

Power**Pointer**

Consider setting up shop in multiple venues, and then put the appropriate merchandise up for sale in each one.

Joyner: You recently went on a weekend buying trip. How will you determine what purchases go on eBay, what merchandise goes on your web site, and what goes in your physical store?

Glasure: That comes through education and experience.

This weekend we came back with tons of stuff, including both a 24-foot Ryder truck and a 16-foot trailer full of inventory. A lot of that will go on eBay, particularly certain rare items. EBay's good for two things: liquidation and selling rare collectibles.

Some of this stuff we'll just decide to sell cheaply on eBay because we want to get rid of it. Other items should sell very well on eBay because they are extremely rare. There is also some stuff that I know will sell better on our web site.

Then there's the merchandise that is not worth selling on eBay, or that has a local interest. This will go to the store. If it's heavy and very hard to ship, we'll try to sell that locally at the store.

This gives you some insight into the thought process that goes into making these decisions.

Joyner: Do you have much right of refusal when buying a collection? In other words, can you refuse certain items, or do you pretty much have to buy everything as one package?

Glasure: Normally, we try to be fair and don't cherry-pick. We usually take everything. That's really the only fair way, because what good are you doing for the seller, especially if it's a widow, by taking all the good stuff and leaving her with a bunch of junk that she'll never be able to sell?

Joyner: In addition to your auctions, you also have an online eBay store. How do you stock it with merchandise?

Glasure: We use our eBay store to help sort our auctions and group items in categories to make it easier for customers to buy multiple items from us. We like to lead everyone to our store home page, where they can access our various auctions.

The advantage for us is people will combine their auctions, so they may buy 20 items from us, rather than buying from 20 different people and paying 20 different shipping charges.

PowerPointer

Realize and promote to customers the advantage of buying several items from you at the same time, including the savings realized from lower combined shipping costs.

Joyner: Do you find that many customers wind up buying more than one item from you, either at one time or on a return visit?

Glasure: Oh, yes. All the time. Take a look at our feedback. We're at about 18,000, but our total feedback is around 80,000. So you know every customer is coming back at least four times.

Joyner: How do you accomplish that? Is there something in particular that you do at Dan's Train Depot that helps to generate repeat business?

Glasure: It's a combination of letting our customers get to know us, giving them great service, and providing excellent packing. We also list a number of similar type items in any given week to appeal to specific collector niches. We may offer a hundred things that a particular type of collector would be interested in at one time because that way they have a number of things to browse through.

Let's say we get G Gauge trains in. In one week, we'll list a lot of G Gauge trains for auction. The collectors really start surfing because they want a bunch of this stuff. And once they bid on something, they keep coming back to see what else we have for sale.

Joyner: For one of my previous books, *The eBay Millionaire*, I interviewed a seller who specialized in vintage movie posters and photos. And he took the same approach. One week he might auction off only John Wayne items to appeal to fans of The Duke and his movies, for instance. He said it was a great way to tap into collectors' passions and generate repeat business.

Glasure: Another thing I've always done, and something I preach to people, is I buy on eBay myself. That way you get to learn what your habits are (habits that are probably shared by other buyers). For example, I'm always more intrigued by a collection or a number of interesting things that I can get from one person that I can trust. I don't have time to fool around buying a bunch of little stuff here and there from multiple sellers.

Power**Pointer**

The best way to learn how to be a better eBay seller is by also being a regular eBay buyer.

Joyner: Is there anything else you've learned as a buyer that has helped you as a seller?

Glasure: I'm irritated if an item is not shipped promptly or well. I get mad if I don't receive any e-mail correspondence, or there's no phone number listed for the merchant, or they don't take PayPal.

Joyner: I presume that early on you identified those as areas in which you would focus your customer service efforts.

Glasure: We've refined our customer service with experience. We try not to become complacent. We always try to learn. We try to take our customers' input, and we attempt to look at what our competitors are doing to determine whether we're lagging behind in any certain area.

Joyner: Given that you sell unique items, and not commodities like books or DVD players, how much time goes into the creation of every auction ad? And how do you minimize the time that you have to spend on creating auction ads without sacrificing quality?

Glasure: We try to streamline, but we don't cut corners on photos. Oftentimes, we'll take 10 photos of each item.

We try to list similar things at any given time so the photographer can create an assembly line and kind of zip along.

We've minimized the time we spend on auction creation on the back end. For example, we've had computer scripts written to where the 300 or so photos we download from our digital camera are automatically resized and cropped. The computer also automatically numbers and saves each photo for uploading.

Power**Pointer**

Streamline the process of loading merchandise into your eBay listings, and take several pictures of each item to get the most optimal shot.

Joyner: That must save a tremendous amount of time. What is the software that you had written specifically for your business?

Glasure: It's custom work that took a long time to get adapted and working correctly. It's not something you can buy off the shelf.

Joyner: Do you use any off-the-shelf digital cameras and equipment?

Glasure: Yes and no. We focus on our lighting, and we're constantly striving to improve that. We have a photo booth. We're using a real good Sony camera right now.

Joyner: But it's not a $10,000 camera?

Glasure: No, though I would pay for such a camera if there was a need for it. We even tried some of the higher-end cameras and found that they were wonderful for taking one photograph at a time, but they didn't suit our needs. We discovered we needed a camera that could take more shots quicker, since it's almost like an assembly line.

Power**Pointer**

> You don't need an expensive, fancy camera to take effective photos for eBay.

Joyner: How many people do you have working for you?

Glasure: Right now there are six, counting myself. I used to have 13 employees, but that created too many headaches. We ran into workers' compensation issues. We found that we were better off streamlining our staff and maybe not growing sales quite as much, but rather focusing more on the profit margin.

Joyner: You bring up an interesting point about being in business for yourself, something many eBay sellers might want to think about. Once you have a certain number of employees, you have to buy workers' compensation insurance and provide other kinds of benefits, all of which can be expensive. What are some of the unexpected costs that you've encountered as a businessperson?

Glasure: There are a lot of expenses people don't factor into their business plans. An accountant is one. Then there's unemployment and workers' compensation insurance, which becomes an issue in our state after the fifth employee. (Some states require it starting with the first hire.)

I think it's more important to emphasize that you must approach eBay like a business if you want it to be a business. If you just want to sell a few things at home that you find at garage sales, that's great. But if you really want this to be a growing business, then you'd better treat it like one.

Power**Pointer**

Never underestimate the costs involved in keeping your business up and running.

Joyner: At what point did you realize that your eBay venture was going to be a real business?

Glasure: I think at the point we spent $27,000 and put a second mortgage on the house is the time we viewed it as something serious enough that it would become a full-time business.

Joyner: You've been able to maintain the same level of revenue with half the staff. How have you managed to increase sales without increasing expenses?

Glasure: By streamlining cash flow and trying to pinpoint where we're the most profitable, as well as trying to focus on the areas where we do well and dropping some of the areas where we don't.

At one point, we branched into remote-control cars, slot cars, and various things. For a while, we were buying out hobby shops instead of estates. The problem is we ended up buying a bunch of stuff that had been picked over. These stores had their going-out-of-business sales and then what we got was a whole bunch of junk. These items take longer to sell.

Joyner: Some people actually think that if you're a merchant on eBay you don't necessarily have to spend much money on Web development or marketing or advertising. They don't want to spend anything beyond their eBay and PayPal fees. But that's not your philosophy. You support making financial investments that will help your company stand out from the competition on eBay.

Glasure: It's like being in a mall. Just because you're paying rent to be there doesn't mean you won't spend money on advertising. You still need to make yourself stand out from the other stores in the mall that sell the same thing. On eBay, you've got to still set yourself apart from everyone else.

At one time, eBay offered co-op advertising dollars. We ran a bunch of really expensive full-page ads in trade magazines, and eBay kicked back 25 percent of the ad cost. Now you're pretty much on your own.

Power**Pointer**

Think of being on eBay as if you are operating in a mall. You still have to advertise and do other activities to attract buyers to your store because you're competing with many other outlets selling the exact same merchandise.

Joyner: You've also worked with a private Web design firm to jazz up your company web site and your auction templates, haven't you?

Glasure: Making our store more presentable, making it easier to browse our items—those types of things have been very beneficial for us.

Joyner: You advocate spending money when necessary, but you also keep tight control of your costs. For example, you use a subscription-based auction management solution instead of one that takes a cut of every sale you make on eBay. Do you have some other strategies or tricks you can share with regard to controlling your eBay costs and your fees? How do you keep expenses manageable so that your profitability is higher?

Glasure: We always use gallery listings, because it gives our auctions more exposure. We don't do reserve auctions, which cost more. And we try to zero in on items that are more profitable.

We've found that items worth less than $10 are not worth it for us no matter what they are because by the time I pay someone to take pictures, list, pack, and do all the various things required to make the sale, it's just not profitable. So we instead try to focus on items that will sell for $10 and up.

I think knowing your competition is important, too. A lot of these rules are just basic business rules. I didn't start out as a business major or somebody who knew all these things, but I was willing to ask and learn and I happened to find people who would help. Some of what I learned was just gathered through trial and error.

I think people starting up a business have to face these same issues. You're going to have your ups and downs, but you must be willing to treat it like a business and you've got to continually educate yourself. The advantage of eBay is it is kind of like a springboard where you can start out small. You don't have to buy a bricks-and-mortar store. You don't have to pay $3,000 a month for rent and $1,000 a month for electricity. You can start in your basement or your home office and see how you do and hopefully grow at a steady pace.

Joyner: Have there been any mistakes you made along the way that you don't mind sharing?

Glasure: I've had other people ask that question and I never really have a good answer because obviously there are lots of them.

Joyner: Have you ever bought a collection that turned out to be a dud, for instance?

Glasure: You know, there have been a few times we bought things that seemed like a good deal but weren't within our area of expertise, and we really did very poorly on them.

Joyner: Presumably, you've gotten better at that with experience.

Glasure: We're to the point now where we can look at a warehouse full of stuff and in about two hours have a pretty good idea how much money is sitting there just by looking around and getting a feel for it and knowing what it is even without counting everything.

Joyner: Do you use just the eBay Marketplace Research tools or offerings from third-party companies to determine how much a particular item might sell for?

Glasure: We haven't really used that stuff much. The problem is they're not always an accurate guide, especially for collectibles. For example, let's say you have X item that sold for $20, $40, and $60. Was it a $20 item from a seller with zero feedback? Was it damaged? Was there no box? Was it poorly painted? You can't always glean that type of information simply by looking at past sales data.

Joyner: That's a good point that I don't think any seller has ever made to me. It sounds like some of this Marketplace Research data is better suited to merchants who are selling new items versus collectibles because there are so many variables when it comes to the condition of collectibles and the reputation of the seller.

Are there any other insights you can share with eBay entrepreneurs?

Glasure: I'm a big proponent of putting together a business plan.

Joyner: Did you have one in the beginning?

Glasure: No, but that's why I'm a big proponent of it. We have a professor here who kind of took a liking to us and really helped me a lot. He has a lot of letters behind his name and is a university business professor. He's given me textbooks, which I've read, and helped me learn how to put together a business plan. At this point, before I'll take on a new project or even a new subproject, I'll always put it to a business plan.

Power**Pointer**

Step one in starting a successful company is to write a comprehensive and well-thought-out business plan.

Joyner: How do you think that helps you? And as a second part to that question, how do you think things would have been different for your company in the beginning had you realized then the importance of having business plan?

Glasure: The business plan does a couple of things. It's like an overgrown budget, in that it really helps you see your expenses. It also gives you some long-term goals that you can look back on and stick with. In that way, it helps you to set up your business and chart its growth in stages.

I think if we'd had a business plan earlier we might have had a little clearer focus and we wouldn't have strayed into some of these side businesses that really kind of hurt us.

But the biggest benefit of a business plan when you're starting is to help you count the costs.

We were fortunate in that we built our online business years ago when you could throw anything on eBay and it would sell. I think if I had started the same way now, we would not have done very well at all.

Joyner: Do you get the sense in your networking, as you talk to people who are selling on eBay or who want to, that many eBay entrepreneurs have business plans?

Glasure: I think the successful ones that last do. And I think all these fly-by-nights don't.

In other words, the most successful merchants write a plan and stick with it. Business plans not only help you to crystallize what your business is all about, but they also allow you to clarify your goals and hold yourself accountable for reaching them. There are many good primers on how to write business plans available both online and at your local library.

Remember, an eBay business is just that—a business. You need to prepare for your success online the same way you would for any other commercial operation, and that means starting out with a clear and well-thought-out written plan.

Like Glasure, it would also be smart to hook up with a mentor, who can serve as an adviser and guide along the way. In doing so, you will profit from your mentor's experience while avoiding some of the costly mistakes that can be so detrimental to your bottom line.

5

Connie Gray

Estate Treasure by Byrum

Connie Gray discovered her professional passion fairly late in her career, around the time that most people start thinking about retirement.

Twenty-some years into her job as a nurse at an ophthalmology practice, she got bitten by the antiques bug. On weekends, Gray would hit the local auction circuit hoping to bid her way to prosperity at neighborhood estate sales. She then rented booths at several antiques malls throughout central Indiana, where she lives, and stocked them with each weekend's estate-sale bounty.

Gray's husband viewed his wife's sideline business as little more than a weekend hobby. But that was before Gray learned about a web site called eBay and turned a $13 estate auction investment into a $657 profit. This was enough money to make both husband and wife take notice.

Eventually Gray, who started selling on eBay in 1998 under the user ID byrum, left her nursing job to sell on the online auction site full time. Now she is a member of the fraternity of professional eBay sellers who together complete more than $1 billion worth of transactions on the site every year—what I call The eBay Billionaires' Club.

Gray continues to focus on the antiques and collectibles categories, specifically pottery and glass, ephemera, textiles, silver, quilts, antique frames, and vintage eclectic housewares—"everything but the kitchen sink," in the words of her web site at www.antiquekitchen.com.

When Gray first began selling on eBay, the site was best known as a place to buy collectibles and hard-to-find antiques. As eBay has aged, however, Gray's business has grown to include more brand-new items. Today, eBay's most successful sellers typically deal in brand-new and brand-name products and commodities like computers, music, and movies. Despite the ever-changing marketplace, Gray has experienced continued success and sales growth while marketing used and unique items. Drawing from her own vast experience and using tools like eBay's Marketplace Research, Gray has managed to increase her average selling price over the years, while reducing her listing fees and other costs of doing business.

One important lesson that Gray has learned is that having a bigger business doesn't necessarily equate to having a more profitable one. Once upon a time, she had several employees working for her. But she has since streamlined operations after realizing how much expenses like workers' compensation insurance cut into her profits. "I had to pay anywhere from $800 to $1,500 a year just for the privilege of having an employee," she says. "And that was just too much."

Estate Treasure by Byrum now has only two employees—Gray and her husband, who is retired from an engineering career. This goes to show that you don't need a big staff to run a profitable online business.

"For my husband and me, it's sort of fun to do something together for the first time in our lives," says Gray, noting that her spouse has a much higher opinion of her company now than he once did. "He was an engineer and worked in a factory for years, and our lives were totally opposite. But now, we sort of like the same things, so that's fun."

An active member of the Professional eBay Sellers Alliance (PeSA), Gray in this chapter offers advice for achieving success in eBay's more unique categories. In her case, the secret is buying from suppliers she can trust, turning merchandise quickly, using Marketplace Research to identify the best sellers in every category, fee management, and accepting occasional losses as a necessary cost of doing business.

Joyner: It seems that most PowerSellers who have been really successful tend to sell commodity-type items. That's not what you're doing. Everything you sell is unique, and mostly antiques. How did you get started in the eBay business, and how do you sustain it selling these types of items?

Gray: I am a registered nurse. I worked in the same field of ophthalmology for 26 years. About three years before I stopped working, I became interested in antique booths in antiques malls. I started buying a few things here and there and selling them through various antique booths. That went on for a year or so.

It just so happened that eBay was gaining momentum in that same time period. One of my patients said, "Don't you know about eBay?" Of course, that was a foreign term; I had no idea what it was. By the time I got home, I couldn't even remember what the word was to look it up.

Months went by before that patient came in again and told me about eBay once more. I think that time I wrote down the name.

In the meantime, in order to stock the booths, I started going to estate auctions. At one of those auctions, very early on, I bought a radio for $13. I decided to try selling it on eBay and it sold for $670.

Joyner: What kind of radio was it?

Gray: It was very rare Bakelite, and it was blue. At that time, I didn't even have a digital camera; I actually used my 35-millimeter camera, and took the film to town to get it developed.

Joyner: Did you have the photos burned onto a CD?

Gray: No. I brought the pictures home and scanned them.

Joyner: When you bought that radio for $13, did you have any idea you'd make such a tidy profit?

Gray: I had an inkling. But the thing I haven't told you is that I had no history—zero—in antiques. I really didn't have an inbred appreciation for anything vintage or older.

Growing up, everything in our home was new, and it was only there because we needed it for one immediate purpose or another. We never treasured old things. Even now, I try to get my mother interested in some older items, and she says, "I don't like old things. I like new stuff."

I was short on history, and that really was a handicap. But I definitely had been around long enough to know that there was just something special about that radio.

At that time, I think I probably knew the term Bakelite and the value of the brand, but I didn't know enough to realize that the blue color was unusually valuable. But I did know enough that I waited for it to come up for bid. It was one of the very last things that sold in a box lot that day, and it was just thrown in there with everything else. I was willing to wait around all day to buy that box.

Of course, I didn't have a clue it would sell for so much. That first eBay sale was followed with other successes, though not necessarily that grand.

Before long, I found myself staying up until 1 a.m. working on my eBay business. I'd have to force myself to go to sleep and then get up and go to work in the morning.

Joyner: So, you moonlighted for a while. What was it like once you finally quit your day job and devoted yourself full-time to eBay?

Gray: For the first three or four years, I probably worked over 80 hours a week. I was so excited and passionate. I had to force myself to go to sleep at night, and I couldn't wait to get up in the morning. I just lived and breathed this business.

Joyner: Had you ever had a job that excited you so much?

Gray: Probably not. I suppose when I first went to work as a nurse, there was some of that level of excitement. But now I had this other life at home that I had to give up to go to work.

It wasn't even a conscious part of my decision to leave nursing, but I used to laugh because working with patients can be challenging. I used to say, "Oh, just give me a computer and lock me in a room. I'll be so happy; I won't have to deal with patients."

But that was unbelievably good training for what I do now because customers are no less demanding. And you don't get to talk with them face-to-face, so you have to over-exude kindness in your e-mails.

Joyner: Once you left your nursing job, did you continue to sell items through local antiques malls?

Gray: I did those for two or three years, while simultaneously selling on eBay. It took that long for me to realize that I could either turn something over in a week on eBay or look at it for six months in a booth. The economics of that seemed ridiculous.

My husband is a cost engineer, and he thinks about that kind of stuff. Another friend who had been a retailer kept saying, "It's turnover. It's all about turnover."

You can't hold the merchandise; you've got to turn it over. The faster you turn it over, regardless of whether the profit is less than you expected, the better for your business.

At least that was the thinking of my husband and friend. Over time, I just decided I'd be willing to take a little less than what I thought an item may be worth just to keep the merchandise moving. My goal is to have zero inventory.

PowerPointer

When you're selling merchandise, the faster you turn it over, the greater your profits.

Joyner: Talk a bit more about the concept of turnover. I think many inexperienced sellers might not understand the importance of turning inventory quickly. Some will relist the same item over and over and over again. How often will you relist an item on eBay?

Gray: I try to never relist items on eBay. Do you know what Marketplace Research is?

Joyner: Yes. It allows you to search past eBay transactions to find out how well particular items have sold and what buyers paid for them.

Gray: When that became available, I knew immediately that it would help my business. Even before Marketplace Research was available, I used completed auction data to see how well a particular item sold. Before, I used to go buy inventory at an auction that I thought was great, yet when I came home and looked it up on eBay, I saw several of the same type of item that hadn't sold in the last two weeks. Right away, I would say, "I've already wasted the money to buy this. Am I going to waste more money to list it, just so I can say I listed it?" I learned really quickly that this is stupid.

Now I constantly use Marketplace Research. It's not a perfect system, but now it has significantly reduced the number of items I buy only to find that they haven't sold well historically on eBay.

Let's go back to your question about when I relist. If I buy an item and notice on Marketplace Research that it hasn't sold, I won't list those items on eBay at all. I turn the merchandise over right then, straight to another auction house. I have sort of a back-end auction house I send stuff to.

If an item is not moving to sell, I do not waste my time trying to auction it on eBay. I've already wasted money buying it, and I'm not going to spend any more time with it.

Power**Pointer**

Use eBay's Marketplace Research area to figure out which items are most likely to sell best.

Joyner: Is this back-end auction house more of a traditional auction? Or is it another online auction marketplace?

Gray: It's not online. It's just a local place that will take my leftovers. Usually, I might break even, or I might lose a little money. But again, it's all about just keeping inventory moving.

Other antique dealers who have their houses and garages full can't do that. I think the people who hang on to slow-moving inventory and suffer the most are dealers who were selling antiques long before the Internet became a viable channel.

They cannot let things go for less than the "book" says. Of course, the book means nothing now. Even in the eight short years I've been in business, I have seen a huge difference in sales trends compared to the past.

There's one particular item that I always used to be able to buy for $10 and sell for $50. Now that same thing might sell for $18, or maybe not at all.

My notion is that in the beginning people thought these things were rare. Now there are so many sellers offering the same item online, buyers know very few things are truly rare. Anybody can find the item they want on eBay anytime, and usually within a range of $10 to $20.

Joyner: Has that realization affected what you buy? In your example of that $10 item that you could always sell for $50, do you still stock it, knowing you can now only sell it for just $18?

Gray: No. In fact, I very recently passed that particular item up in an antique store. I just didn't bother with it, because it wasn't worth the effort.

Let me be more specific on my relisting strategy. If I have an unsuccessful auction where an item doesn't sell, I look at all available data from auctions of identical items and ask myself, "Did I really think this should have sold?" If I really believe the item is unique and should have sold, and the Marketplace Research supports that, I will relist it once.

If an item doesn't sell the second time, and if I still am confident that this is a great thing, I will put it my eBay store. But it has to be something that I know somebody is going to want at this price.

PowerPointer

Try not to relist an item more than once. (Your goal should be to list items so they'll sell the first time and won't have to be relisted.)

Joyner: We've talked about your selling and buying strategies. What about pricing? Do you have a rule of thumb that you follow when pricing items for an online auction?

Gray: Nothing specific. I've tried everything from the penny opening bid to the 99-cent model to just asking myself what I think an item is really worth. Right now, I'm somewhere in between.

I have a PeSA friend whom I respect greatly. We talked one day for about an hour about my business. At that time, I felt like you had to follow the same opening bid model for all of your auctions. It never really crossed my mind that I could do a little bit of each, which sounds a bit ridiculous now.

Anyway, my friend said, "Why don't you do a certain percentage using the various pricing models?" So I did.

My thinking is that there are some people who search for penny or 99-cent auctions. They're not looking for anything in particular, but they're searching at that price level. This does bring me some customers. While I didn't want to give up that business, I was losing too much money listing everything that way.

For a short time—perhaps two months—I started the bidding for every one of my auctions at a penny. My traffic increased phenomenally, and profits actually went up. But I sold some really good stuff for a penny that I paid a fair amount of money for. So I decided I didn't want to do that anymore.

Another PeSA connection suggested the 99-cent model, which gives you better bid increments. I had never thought about that before.

Joyner: By better bid increments, do you mean that with each bid the price rises higher and quicker if you start the listing at 99 cents?

Gray: Right. That's so important and it can certainly affect your profitability.

With that in mind, this is my current strategy: If I buy an item for very little money—and I can do that because I purchase a lot of box lots—I will start those items at 99 cents. I might pay $20 for a box lot with 50 things in there. I'm not going to stand to lose a lot of money by pricing those items at 99 cents. I do that in order to generate traffic for my auctions, but only on a limited number of things, maybe 20 percent. On the rest, I set a starting price that I think is fair for the item.

PowerPointer

There's no need to always stick with just one pricing strategy. You can change your approach, depending on what you think will work best for a particular item.

Joyner: A lot of the items you sell are fragile, and antiques run the gamut in size. Do you try to stick with smaller, nonbreakable items just to make shipping easier for yourself?

Gray: One of my big problems is shipping, in that size and weight vary so dramatically with what I sell. I'm so envious of people who sell TVs or shirts and ties—things that always weigh the same amount.

Every time I'm sitting at an auction deciding whether I want to bid on an item I'm thinking, "Do I really want to work that hard? Yes, it's a good price. But do I really want to work that hard to get it packed and shipped?" The ultimate decision on whether to buy lies in the item price, size, weight, shippability, and such.

Still, in spite of ourselves, we do ship some large things. We ship small tables. One of our biggest-selling items, actually, is antique picture frames. Those things can be huge when they are packed because of the glass.

Shipping concerns are never out of my mind. I won't make a purchase without weighing the pros and cons of shipping the item, though you don't have a lot of time to consider these variables when you're sitting in an auction.

Power**Pointer**

Among the variables to consider when deciding whether to stock an item for sale: How easily can it be shipped? After all, shipping charges can sometimes cost more than the merchandise itself, instantly turning off any potential buyers.

Joyner: Do you have a preferred shipping provider?

Gray: We do. We have a UPS daily pickup.

Our shipping costs went up 30 percent last year, but our sales were just about the same as in the previous year. That was a horrible red flag, and my accountant didn't like it, either. I knew that we had to do something to reduce shipping costs. Part of the increase, of course, was due to the rising price of gasoline.

I've recently been in negotiations with UPS and FedEx to try to come up with a better solution. But there really isn't one. Customers still want to pay what they paid two or three years ago.

When eBay began including estimated shipping costs in every auction, that really hurt the people like me because when you indicate that it might cost $50 to ship a picture frame to Oregon or Indiana, bidders are not going to even look at it.

Joyner: It's interesting that you mention picture frames, and specifically the high cost of shipping large pieces of glass. I recently purchased a large frame for a painting from an online company. Because I was framing a canvas, I just needed the frame, not the glass. But I noticed on the web site that this company doesn't even offer glass with its frame kits. They ship only acrylic sheets, because of the high price of shipping glass. Now I understand why they do that. The shipping costs are so prohibitive.

Gray: That's true. Unfortunately, my customers want the glass, especially if it's old glass. It just kills them if the glass gets broken in transit, which is another problem we have to deal with.

We have the unique problem that our stuff can't be replaced. So we go overboard with padding and packaging materials when shipping fragile items. Of course, that makes the package so massive, it costs a fortune to ship. But we don't want it to get damaged.

Joyner: Unlike many sellers, you don't like to use shipping calculators in your auctions. You prefer to charge a flat rate for shipping. Why?

Power**Pointer**

When selling heavy or bulky merchandise, consider offering flat-rate shipping, in order to ease the minds of buyers concerned about how much it will cost to have the item delivered.

Gray: Every time I write an ad, I weigh the item, I state in the ad text what the item weighs, and I estimate what I think it's going to take to ship that item safely.

I occasionally will integrate a shipping calculator into my auctions. But the calculators sometimes overstate the cost of the shipping and that can drive bidders away. I'd much rather use a flat rate, and I do probably 80 or 90 percent of the time. But with flat-rate shipping, sometimes I lose money.

Joyner: Information about shipping is just one component that sellers should include in their eBay ads. From your perspective as an antiques dealer, can you talk about other important components to an auction listing? Do you have to write those differently than, say, if you were selling a computer?

Gray: You do. I suppose the most critical part of it is that because of search-engine optimization, you've got to get the right keywords in the ad.

Today, I just wrote an ad for a cute little Florida souvenir belt that I got for nothing. All the way around the belt are these little two-inch pieces of aluminum that are actually woven into the leather. Every one of them has a different picture on it.

If I just wrote the description like many others, I would say, "Here's a belt. It's made of aluminum and leather. It's a Florida souvenir." I'd give the dimensions, and it would probably sell.

But what I've done to reach more bidders and maximize my selling price is describe every little picture on the aluminum insets. I wrote that it has flamingos, a girl skiing, a map of Florida, and so forth.

Therefore, I've got all those keywords that somebody might be looking for covered. If they search for "Florida flamingo," they're going to come to that ad.

PowerPointer

Include as many details as possible about your items in the written description, so you can hit on all of the possible keywords a potential buyer might use when searching for the product. You may also want to include some common misspellings at the bottom of the page, just in case some bad spellers are looking for what you have to offer.

Joyner: Any other tips?

Gray: I include commonly misspelled words appropriately at the bottom of the auction ad, when necessary. I list the size and condition of an item, and I always tell the truth, no matter whether it is good or bad.

Right now, for instance, I have two pieces of Roseville pottery on eBay. One I started at 99 cents and another at $49.99. The reason is that one piece of pottery has several damaged spots that I didn't see when I bought it. I knew it had a chip, but I didn't know it had two chips and a crack. So in the title for that item, I even included the word "damaged." I don't want to tease bidders, then have them get to the bottom of the ad and discover the item is in terrible condition. You've just wasted their time and ticked them off. And you're not going to sell an item that way.

Power**Pointer**

Be honest and straightforward with your item listings. If something is damaged or not in good working order, be upfront about it.

Joyner: EBay now gives shoppers lots of ways to search for items. For example, they can search for keywords in the auction title or in the description, among a myriad of other ways. Just how important is the auction title? Do you still need to include keywords in the title? Or is it sufficient to include them only in the item description?

Gray: I weigh every word, and even the order of words in the title. I think titles are still critical because I always think I'm dealing with a novice. I think of the shopping experience through their eyes, and they may not have a clue of how to search for keywords in the description, as well as in the title.

Joyner: Good photographs are another key to eBay success. How many photographs might you include in an ad for a unique item?

Gray: Anywhere from one to twelve. The average is four or five.

Joyner: You get most of your inventory from live auctions and estate sales. Any tips for finding and buying merchandise in these venues that can later be resold at a profit on eBay?

Gray: In the beginning, I had friends who had been in the antiques business for a long time and they would not bid against me at auctions.

They were trying to be nice. Then I would do that for my friends. But it became confusing to keep track of all the people who were your friends whom you were bidding against.

Joyner: So, if I'm reading you right, you're saying that you have to put personal feelings aside and be competitive?

Gray: You just have to close your eyes and direct your attention straight ahead, at the auctioneer. You don't look around to see who is bidding against you. You can't.

Joyner: Sounds like you have to balance being a nice person and a smart businesswoman. But that's a lesson all readers have to learn. Is Bill Gates thinking about Michael Dell when he's negotiating deals for Microsoft?

Gray: I don't think so.

Joyner: Do you travel the country going to auctions and estate sales?

Gray: Sometimes we'll drive out of town to Illinois or Ohio, but often when we come home, we feel like the auctioneer might not have been honest. I've never come home from one of those excursions feeling 100 percent good about it, even though we might get some things and didn't have to fight against our regular competitors.

A lot of our success has to do with the auctioneers that we choose to buy from. The time I got stung and bought a reproduction item that I thought was authentic, we were traveling in Kentucky. People got ripped off a ton that day because of an unscrupulous auctioneer. But around here, we know our auctioneers. Generally speaking, we're standing in the front yard of the house of somebody who was 90 years old and died.

Power**Pointer**

It's not necessary to travel the world looking for quality merchandise. Sometimes the best stuff is in your own backyard.

Joyner: Do you even bother with garage sales?

Gray: Almost never. I stopped going about four years ago. One Saturday, I spent four hours, and spent a total of 50 cents on merchandise. Yet, I wasted a lot more in gas driving around. There's something not right about that.

Joyner: You have a 100 percent positive feedback score on eBay. How have you accomplished that?

Gray: At first, I wanted to be totally honest and grade everyone on the total aspect of the sale, but it didn't take long before I received a retaliatory negative response. Bam! That taught me a lesson. It so happened that he used profanity in his comment, and so I was able to get the negative comment removed.

Joyner: You were lucky.

Gray: It was a blessing.

Bad feedback is more damaging to a seller than a buyer. Before someone makes a purchase, they may spend a lot of time studying someone's feedback—that is, going to see if they have negative feedback, why they got it, and how they responded to it.

Now I only leave feedback if it has been left for me.

Feedback for the customer is not just about whether they paid as promised. It is about whether they responded to me appropriately if there were a problem. I can make mistakes, and I always do whatever it takes to please the customer. Sometimes if a customer is dissatisfied, they are on the attack from the first e-mail. It takes a lot to push me to give something other than positive feedback, but I will do it if I am pushed too far.

Joyner: When you do give negative or neutral feedback, do you worry that the buyer will do the same for you?

Gray: No, because I don't leave feedback until they've left it for me.

Power**Pointer**

Keep in mind that leaving buyer feedback is part of the overall customer service offered by your site.

Joyner: Given that it can be retaliatory in nature, should buyers be suspicious of feedback? How much weight should they give to one person's negative comments?

Gray: I still think it carries weight. I know exactly what you're saying, but I'm convinced that over the long haul feedback still matters.

Joyner: I would agree with you. I'm just trying to play devil's advocate a little bit.

Gray: I've heard this question before. I have a friend who loves to antagonize me about the value of feedback. He asks the question, "Why does it even mean anything if people are afraid to say something negative for fear that it will reflect back on them?"

He's right. There are a lot of people out there who deserve negative things that weren't said, and I feel bad about not giving them negative feedback. But I decided that my business was not worth it.

Granted, it takes time to leave feedback for customers, but it can be an important component of your company's overall customer service initiative. While you'll occasionally want to leave negative feedback when you run into a really troublesome customer that you feel others should be aware of, most of the time you'll be saying something nice. And providing such positive feedback for good customers will likely increase their affection for your company, making them more inclined to want to do business with you again in the future.

6

John Wieber

Exel-i

John Wieber was first lured to eBay during his quest for a new computer. But unlike many of the auction site's early devotees, he didn't find any bargains. Quite the contrary. Instead, Wieber, who had visited a number of e-commerce web sites looking for the best deal on a computer, noticed that prices on eBay were often inflated. Thanks to frenzied bidding, refurbished computers sold for more on eBay than on the manufacturers' own web sites.

Though Wieber didn't wind up buying on eBay, he smelled an opportunity. He parlayed his newfound knowledge about the auction marketplace into what is now a multimillion-dollar, multichannel online business called Exel-i. Wieber, an ex–Long Islander (hence the name Exel-i) and former traveling textiles salesman, found his own source for obtaining refurbished laptop computers, bought them, and began reselling the machines on eBay. In those early days, he sold as many as 30 computers a day, clearing about $150 on each one. Before long, Wieber was making more on eBay than at his real job. So, he quit to pursue his e-commerce dream full-time. Within just two years,

Exel-i's eBay sales reached the Platinum PowerSeller range with Wieber booking a $100,000 profit on revenues of $420,000.

Exel-i, which Wieber runs with investor and neighbor Douglas Deist, is now a leading online broker of new and used computers and parts. Annual revenues top $5 million with sales coming from a variety of online channels, including eBay, Amazon, and the company's own web site, www.laptopbroker.com. In addition to working directly with computer equipment manufacturers, the company specializes in asset recovery. That's jargon for a fairly common industry practice. Businesses and government agencies are continually upgrading and replacing their computers and other technical equipment. Quite often, however, the equipment is functional and too good to be trashed. A computer that might be obsolete in an office may be in high demand among home users. That's where asset recovery companies like Wieber's come into the picture.

Exel-i buys or takes in these unwanted technical assets from companies and government entities on consignment. Then, it repairs and resells the items for a profit on eBay and other online channels. The company gets its products from a variety of sources. Products arrive in Exel-i's Gaithersburg, Maryland, warehouse in anything from as-is to shipshape condition. Before listing the computers, mostly laptops, for sale online, warehouse workers inspect and test each machine and technicians perform any repairs necessary to return them to working order.

Exel-i is at a crossroads in its evolution as a company. The business owes its existence to eBay, and indeed Wieber and his partner have earned hundreds of thousands of dollars because of their presence on the auction web site. But the marketplace is changing, due in part to increased competition as well as the increased listing and selling fees imposed by eBay management. Sales made on eBay, though still a significant part of Exel-i's revenues, aren't as profitable as they once were.

That reality has pushed Wieber to dabble in other online marketplaces, specifically Amazon.com and the company's own web sites, where his selling costs aren't as high. Wieber also pushes back against nearly every fee hike that eBay imposes as a way of keeping his profits on the site steady. A few years ago, for example, eBay began charging higher fees for fixed-price listings and those featuring supersized photographs of merchandise. Those two changes alone would have cost Exel-i an estimated $40,000 in additional listing fees every year, thus significantly cutting into profits. Wieber's solution was to stop utilizing those listing upgrades and features.

In the following pages, Wieber talks about how he has kept his business competitive and profitable, despite the changing landscape of eBay. He shares his insights about buying and refurbishing merchandise and preparing it for resale. He even talks about how competitors can help one another by becoming actively involved in networking groups like the Professional eBay Sellers Alliance, what I refer to as The eBay Billionaires' Club. There's a real advantage to sharing and communicating openly with other online merchants, Wieber believes, and his company has benefited from both the give and take of networking.

Joyner: Do you have a technical background in computers, or did you teach yourself those skills as you started selling on eBay?

Wieber: I had a limited technical background, but basically none.

Joyner: So, how did you get into this business?

Wieber: I went shopping for a new computer at different web sites like Compaq, Dell, eBay, and Amazon. I noticed the great variance in prices on the equipment. I said, "What's stopping me from buying the equipment through the cheap web sites and selling it on the expensive ones?" I knew just about nothing about computers at that point. To me they were just a commodity.

Joyner: But you clearly sensed an opportunity. You're now sourcing products from Fortune 500 companies, as well as some pretty big names in the computer manufacturing industry. How were you able to break into this line of business and win over these companies? What did it take to convince them to sell these items to you?

Wieber: I often say that all the bridges we crossed are really no longer there. No one could follow in my footsteps today, because everything on eBay has changed so greatly. To be competitive on eBay in my category now, you have to be able to buy significant quantities of product. You can't just go and spend $5,000 or $10,000 on some equipment, buy it, sell it, and make a profit. You have to get to the point where we are now, where you can spend six figures and up on inventory.

Not too many people just starting out in the basement of their house can afford to do that, which makes it tough.

But by the same token, guys like me are turning over every rock that they can to get their hands on every single piece of equipment possible.

Joyner: It sounds like yours is a pretty competitive business on eBay, making it tougher for someone who's just starting out to build a lucrative, full-time career buying and selling refurbished computers and parts. But I'm sure there are still many lessons that would-be eBay entrepreneurs can learn from your experiences in asset recovery.

In your case, are you buying the merchandise outright from companies? Or do you ever sell anything on a consignment basis?

Wieber: We do a little bit on consignment, but only because of our reputation. Companies know they are going to make more money if they consign products to us. If I have to reach into my own pocket and buy something, I'm not going to pay you as much as you might earn on consignment.

Power**Pointer**

Selling on consignment is a good way to protect your financial position because you don't have to invest in inventory. However, keep in mind that frequently you'll get (or have to give) a bigger cut of the overall take when doing business under this structure.

Joyner: Have you always done it that way, in terms of buying the merchandise outright, or did you sell on consignment in the beginning because of cash flow issues?

Wieber: In our industry, unless you're well-known as a reputable re-seller, no one will consign anything to you. We're talking about $50,000, $100,000, maybe $200,000 worth of equipment. Companies aren't going to trust someone they don't know with that much inventory. Someone is not going to consign you that kind of volume without first coming to look at your facility, running a background check, and knowing everything there is to know about you.

Joyner: That certainly sounds fair. Just to be clear, do you prefer the consignment model for your business, or would you rather buy the inventory outright?

Wieber: It kind of depends. I would say that for the most part it doesn't matter. But it kind of depends on what's involved with the deal, what equipment it is, how fast I think I can turn it, and some other factors as well. Based on those factors, I'll make a judgment call as to what method I prefer.

Joyner: When you're buying equipment to resell, either from the government or from Fortune 500 companies, what are you looking for? Is it important for you to buy in large quantities?

Wieber: I pretty much won't entertain anything unless I can buy at least 100 duplicate items. I want as many tractor-trailer loads as I can get.

Joyner: I would think that might be an evolution in your thinking as your company has grown bigger. Why do you prefer to buy in large quantities?

Wieber: It definitely is an evolutionary thing. The reason I would say 100 is my minimum is because there is a certain amount of time and effort that goes into developing resources to test, diagnose, and repair equipment and parts. It requires a certain amount of labor to compose auction ads, create descriptions, and do the research on the Internet to come up with competitive pricing. By the time you figure all those things into the equation, I can't profitably sell 7 or 15 or 22 of something. It's almost a frightening proposition that someone would put in all of this effort to sell only 10 of something.

Power**Pointer**

When selling commodity-like items, it's generally wise to stock up on as many like products as possible, given the amount of work it takes to create a listing for each one.

Joyner: That certainly makes perfect sense. You want to buy merchandise in large quantities because you have so much investment on the front end. Is it correct to assume that every item in your inventory goes through some kind of diagnostics before you list it for sale?

Wieber: Sure. You can compare it to used cars. Used computers are not very different from used cars. When you sell your vehicle to a used-car dealer, they have to check it, inspect it, and make sure it's safe and okay for resale. We basically do the same thing with computers.

Unfortunately, used computers and used cars are similar in other aspects, too. Yesterday, the engine started fine, but today it's dead. The same thing can happen with used computers: I tried it yesterday and it worked fine, but today it doesn't turn on.

Joyner: How do you assess and grade used computers to make sure that you're selling quality merchandise that will work as the consumer expects it to? Or do you just sell products on an as-is basis?

Wieber: We've tried every different avenue there is. We've tried selling products as is, and we've tried grading every individual product. The solution we've adopted is that all equipment needs to meet a minimum specification. It can be better than this, but it has to have at least a certain level of functionality. Then we'll create a description of the item based on these minimum specifications.

Power**Pointer**

When selling used merchandise, such as computers, establish minimum specifications that the products must meet in order to be in salable condition, and clearly communicate these requirements to buyers so there are no misunderstandings.

Joyner: In other words, some people get exactly what is listed, while others are shipped merchandise that is in better condition that the minimum specification?

Wieber: Right. If you read my feedback, you will see that the vast majority of people report that the product is better than they expected, and they got it fast. A small portion will tell you that the item was pretty much as it was described. And a small percentage will leave negative feedback because they were dissatisfied with their purchase.

Joyner: How much time and money would you spend to repair an item in order to bring it up to the minimum specification level?

Wieber: The answer to that question is in direct relation to how much I paid for it and how much I can sell it for. Maybe I'll buy equipment that needs a lot of work. The only reason I'm buying it is because I'm getting it for a very cheap price. I'm putting labor into it, but the upside is there. I buy some equipment that we have to do barely anything to.

Joyner: Presumably you would pay a little more for equipment that requires few, if any, repairs.

Wieber: Of course. Sometimes a lot more.

Joyner: Do you hire outside contractors to do the repair work on computers? Or do you have people on staff who now do that?

Wieber: I have a staff.

Joyner: How big is your company now? How many employees do you have?

Wieber: We have 14 employees.

Joyner: And how does that shake out? What are their different tasks and responsibilities? How many employees do you have on the tech side, for instance?

Wieber: Basically, most of our resources are spent on hardware repair and refurbishment. Seven of our employees work on computer hardware all day every day. We have two who work in accounting and two who basically deal with online sales and customer service–related issues. We have one and a half employees who are basically software guys who do Web development, software creation, and database work. We also have three warehouse people.

Joyner: Explain what happens when you bring merchandise into your warehouse.

Wieber: It all starts with my inventory procurement process. We usually get a load of equipment packed up in either boxes or skids. If it's grade A equipment, I get an invoice that includes descriptions and conditions of the products. Once the items are shelved, our technical people double-check it before we resell it. If I buy equipment that is grade B, it probably has a little something wrong with it and we need to put some work into it before we can sell it. When we get that equipment, we inspect and repair it. Maybe we see that one computer needs a new keyboard and another needs a hard drive. If we buy grade C equipment, it might have two or three things wrong and we would repair it.

Typically as the grade of equipment goes down, the less information we receive about what's included in that shipment. When we buy grade C equipment, I might get a purchase order that says I'm buying 1,000 incomplete laptops. Our warehouse staff must comb through the entire shipment and note model numbers, check the hard drives, and record the amount of RAM on each machine.

Then, the technician comes over to see whether this laptop has a broken this or bad that, and we might have to replace three or four things, which can become a drag on my technical team.

The reason I'm willing to buy lower-grade equipment is that I get it cheaper and I figure the processing and repair costs into my total price.

I'll even buy products as is if the price is right. I might buy a tractor-trailer load of stuff—computer and office equipment—and have a general idea of what might be on that truck, but I don't know for sure, which can get really interesting.

Joyner: Have you ever purchased a truckload as is and gotten something other than computer equipment?

Wieber: Let's just say I win a lot more than I lose, but there definitely have been some losses. That's the nature of this business. Unless you have pretty deep pockets, you can't even play in it because if you're a new guy and you start out with one of these as is deals and your first load is a bad load, you just might be out of business.

Power**Pointer**

If you plan to buy truckloads of asset recovery merchandise, remember that it can be like winning—or losing—a lottery. Sometimes the items will be in top-grade shape. Other times they will be barely usable, if at all. Most likely they will be somewhere in the middle. It's all part of the risk you take when dealing with this type of merchandise, which is often delivered in bulk by the truckload.

Joyner: The price you are willing to pay for inventory obviously must go down depending on the amount of time and work you'll have to invest in order to return the equipment to sellable condition. But that's not to say you won't buy lower-grade merchandise if the price is right, correct?

Wieber: That's basically it.

Joyner: When you are pricing to sell merchandise online, specifically on eBay, how do you establish the right amount for a particular item? In some categories, sellers will list merchandise starting at 99 cents. But I would think that in a competitive field like computers you wouldn't want to do that because you might end up selling some expensive equipment at a loss.

Wieber: We list a lot of things at a penny only because we know through experience how many of something you can sell without totally segregating your market. The problem is if you're a little guy, you need to turn your inventory very quickly.

Joyner: What you're saying seems to be a little counterintuitive because I hear a lot of retailers on eBay and in the bricks-and-mortar world preaching that you have to turn your merchandise quickly. But you're telling me that's not always the best route to take.

Wieber: No, it's not.

It takes a lot of forecasting and management to be a successful eBay merchant. You need to understand what the value of something is today. You need to understand what the value is going to be tomorrow, and the next day, and probably about 90 to 120 days out, if not six months out.

You have to be able to know if it's going to appreciate or depreciate. You need to know how many of something you can realistically sell in a specific time frame for a specific price. Then you need to put the price into forecasting models and manage your margin.

There is a camp out there that talks about selling more volume. But that usually equates to less margin. Anybody in the world can sell tons and tons and tons of something at a loss. Anybody can. It takes zero effort, zero intelligence to do that. But that's what happens often on eBay.

Power**Pointer**

It's not always about selling as much merchandise as quickly as possible. Sometimes that can be a formula for low margins. Take the time to understand how much your merchandise is worth, and don't be in a rush to get rid of an item, because such impatience may take a bite out of your bottom line.

Joyner: Does eBay help you generate additional sales? And does it help drive business to your web site?

Wieber: Of course it does. Every time I make a sale on eBay that's my customer.

Joyner: What do you do to reach out to customers after they buy from you on eBay?

Wieber: Well, that's difficult. Number one, you have to put some marketing materials in with the product when you ship it. You need to have a good follow-up system, like e-mail that allows you to continue communicating with those customers. Every which way you can possibly follow up and correspond with them, you need to do it.

Power**Pointer**

Always follow up with customers by e-mail and other means. Also, put marketing materials about your company, including other products you sell, in with each shipment.

Joyner: Do you get many repeat customers on eBay? How does your repeat costumer rate on eBay compare to the rate on your web site?

Wieber: Repeat sales on the web site are much better. On eBay, loyalty is usually somewhat limited. If you are competitively priced with someone else and customers have bought from you before, they probably would lean toward buying from you again. But if someone's $3 cheaper, they're going to go buy from someone else.

Joyner: So usually your best way to drive repeat business is to market to customers off of eBay and convince them to buy from you through your web site.

Wieber: Yes.

Joyner: A lot of people spin their wheels trying to generate repeat business on eBay. But it sounds like you're telling me that's a worthless proposition, that if you want someone to buy from you again you need to have your own online channel, specifically your own web site, that you can direct them to.

Wieber: Why would you want to send a customer back to eBay? There is no reason to send them back to eBay. Why would you want to pay eBay a commission for a customer you've already cultivated?

Power**Pointer**

In reality, it's tough to generate repeat business on eBay, because so many shoppers on the site are primarily concerned about price. Therefore, if you have your own web site, try to steer future business through this channel instead. Doing so will also allow you to save on paying eBay fees the next time a customer buys something from you.

Joyner: But a lot of people do that because they don't have enough technical skills, infrastructure, or financial wherewithal to build a web site.

Do you see e-commerce as a growth industry? Particularly, as you've diversified, is there still a lot of growth potential for your business? You're not going to be shopping around for your next job anytime soon, are you?

Wieber: I'm not looking to do that—look for another job—in the immediate future, no. Is there growth in this business? Yes, because we are constantly diversifying and looking for new avenues. But if we were resting all of our success on eBay, it would be a death sentence. Anybody exclusively selling on one venue—whether it's eBay, Amazon, Overstock, whatever—their days are numbered, in my opinion.

Joyner: Why do you say that? A lot of people reading this would argue that some have been very successful selling exclusively on eBay. Take, for example, many of the Titanium PowerSellers I wrote about in my previous book, *The eBay Millionaire.*

Wieber: I would argue that the eBay landscape has changed since many of those people started their businesses. There is a really short supply of success stories from the last 18 months. There are far more death-spiral stories than there are success stories.

Joyner: Do you think that has as much to do with people not really knowing how to run businesses and getting in over their heads? Or can the challenges be attributed to the ever-increasing competitiveness of marketplaces like eBay or Amazon?

Wieber: I would say it's probably an even mix of the two. There are a lot of people in business for themselves who should not be. By the same token, eBay, in particular, is not making it easy for people to make money because they keep raising fees and putting more challenges in place, making it absolutely as difficult as possible to make money. Things cost more to sell on eBay now than they did a few years ago and there is absolutely no reason whatsoever for that. That's because eBay management made mistake after mistake after mistake in the last five years and lost or wasted billions and billions of dollars. That's the reason they want you to pay more to sell on the site.

Joyner: It's also the reason that books like this are so valuable, since they can help aspiring entrepreneurs avoid some of the pitfalls that cause others to fail, while jump-starting their knowledge by many years.

Turning to another topic, because of some software integration issues, you've recently stopped accepting PayPal, which is the preferred payment method of many eBay buyers and sellers. Do you think you are going to lose business by not accepting PayPal?

Wieber: My thought on the matter is I will get less for my items on eBay. But I truly believe that will be outweighed by having to spend less money to manage PayPal. We accept credit cards directly. We accept other electronic payment methods as well. We accept cashier's checks. We accept money orders. We accept Google Checkout. If someone's not going to pay us, it's not because there are not enough opportunities to do so.

If they don't want to give me their credit card directly, they can pay with Google, or they can pay through some other method. If they want to give us their credit card details directly, they can pay with their credit card.

Power**Pointer**

Give customers plenty of options to pay for merchandise, including credit cards, cashier's checks, and services such as Google Checkout.

Joyner: You sure do have lots of options. Google Checkout is still a relatively new service and many people may not yet have experienced paying for online purchases that way. Given that it's a service provided by Google, a name people generally trust, I suspect it could gain popularity quickly and become a real competitor to PayPal. What's your view on that?

Wieber: Anything Google does they typically do well. They are going up against a pretty significant competitor with PayPal on eBay. By the same token, Google is going to be a significant competitor at some point. Lord knows they have the resources.

Joyner: And a great reputation, too.

Wieber: Indeed. I would say the potential is there for Google to take a significant portion of PayPal's business, or at the very least really stunt PayPal's growth.

Joyner: I want to ask you about eBay stores. Do you sell much merchandise through the store format? I know that for a while some bigger sellers were migrating a lot of their merchandise to eBay stores because of the lower fee structure. EBay has subsequently raised fees, making it more expensive to sell items in an eBay store. Are eBay stores a significant part of your business, or do most of your sales come from auctions?

Wieber: We've sold very little in stores.

EBay showed signs of making stores significant when it changed the site's primary search results to include items sold through the store format in those listings. As a result, for a brief blink in time, stores were very lucrative.

EBay quickly circled the wagons and unplugged that search response. Subsequently, it raised the fees significantly to list merchandise for sale in an eBay store.

Joyner: That's one of the complaints I hear from both buyers and sellers—that it's so difficult to find items that are being sold exclusively in eBay stores. Store inventory items usually don't show up in basic eBay search results; consumers wanting to find those items must search for them a specific way.

Wieber: The only way shoppers will find stuff in stores is if they're searching for an item that is very unique.

Joyner: I know that a lot of merchants have used their eBay stores to market up-sell type items, such as accessories to complement their primary products. If you're selling cars, for example, you might offer car covers in your eBay store.

Wieber: It's not really an efficient way to even do that. The efficient way to do what you're talking about is through cross-selling. Get people through your checkout and encourage them to add items there.

Joyner: Do you do a lot of cross-selling?

Wieber: Yes, but it's difficult for us to manage. If eBay was the be-all and end-all of our business, we would have all of that mastered. But because it's not our only channel of distribution, we only put so many resources into managing it. On occasion, we attempt to cross-sell merchandise, but it's not utterly important to us.

Joyner: You are a pretty vocal and active member of the Professional eBay Sellers Alliance, or what I like to call The eBay Billionaires' Club. Why is it important for you to be a member of that organization? Are you still learning things from other sellers now when you go to PeSA meetings? Or are you at the point in your career where you're doling out advice to newer, less-experienced sellers?

Wieber: Every time I get together with them I learn something. There is an endless pool of people who can help you.

I would say now I probably give help more than I get. But it wasn't always that way. I was probably one of the first 50 members, so I've been benefiting from the networking since the beginning. I now have an obligation to see it through and help other eBay sellers.

Joyner: From my experiences interviewing various PeSA members, I've gotten the impression that this is a group of people who are very willing to help others in the field. They're not going to give their competitors a blueprint to knock them out of the business, but people are really willing to share practical advice on the best auction management software and any number of things like that. Is that your experience as well?

Wieber: Absolutely.

I was sitting at eBay Live! chatting with two of my biggest competitors. These are the guys I go toe-to-toe with every day, but we have some similar problems. Sometimes only a direct competitor can understand the problems you are encountering.

There's no doubt that Wieber is frustrated by how some things work at eBay, despite having built such a successful company through the site. But he knows what he's talking about, and has clearly made the case for why you should try to expand your business beyond eBay. If you're just starting out, you don't have to make the leap to what's known as multichannel online marketing right away. Nevertheless, that goal should be part of your overall business plan.

Expanding your horizons by selling through other online venues, including your own web site, will significantly increase your presence and pool of potential buyers, while allowing you to save on selling fees (especially when folks purchase items from you directly).

For more information on how to master the art of multichannel online marketing, I encourage you to check out my book *The Online Millionaire* (John Wiley & Sons, 2007), which deals exclusively with this topic. You'll also hear from a number of successful merchants who have done just that and are reaping the rewards on Amazon.com, Yahoo!, Overstock.com and the various competing auction sites beyond eBay.

For more information on the topic of multichannel online marketing, you can also visit my web site at www.theonlinemillionaire.com.

7

Amy Mayer and Ellen Navarro

ExpressDrop

Business partners Amy Mayer and Ellen Navarro blended two popular concepts to create their successful eBay venture, ExpressDrop.

The two young women, who met as coworkers at a clothing boutique, opened Chicago's first eBay drop-off store in 2004, in essence becoming professional trading assistants. Trading assistants are experienced eBayers who sell for others on the site. In the case of Express-Drop, clients bring their unwanted merchandise to the store and Navarro and Mayer post it for auction, dealing with all the hassles inherent in selling on eBay. For their effort, the pair charges a commission ranging upwards of 32 percent of the selling price.

But ExpressDrop isn't your typical eBay drop-off store. In addition to selling for individuals, Mayer and Navarro also sell merchandise for other businesses, specifically upscale clothing boutiques that need to get rid of out-of-season and slow-moving merchandise. In that way, the two entrepreneurs are exploiting another lucrative inventory channel on eBay—overstock merchandise purchased either outright or consigned for retailers and manufacturers.

Mayer and Navarro have a few rules when it comes to accepting merchandise for consignment. While they specialize in designer clothing, they will take items in any category as long as they're convinced the merchandise will sell for $50 or more on eBay. Most ExpressDrop customers don't incur any expense unless their item sells. The company's service includes a free seven-day auction listing. Items listed under this arrangement open with a starting bid of $19.99 and include a gallery photo.

Consigners wanting more control over pricing can opt for ExpressDrop's premium listing package, which costs $14.99. The money buys a 10-day auction on eBay, and the consigner has the option of setting the opening bid price and including either a reserve or Buy It Now price for the auction.

No matter what package they choose, customers consigning their merchandise through ExpressDrop are responsible for paying all eBay final-value and PayPal fees, in addition to the drop-off store's minimum commission of $15.99. So, on a $50 item a consigner would get $30.20, and on a $1,000 item the consigner's share would be $655.14.

In two years, ExpressDrop has grown to include two stores, the flagship store in Chicago and a franchise in the Chicago suburb of Wilmette. The company's annual revenues are more than $1 million. Mayer and Navarro have plans of expanding the business by selling other franchises and increasing the number of boutique liquidation accounts they handle.

The pair, who also teach classes to people interested in learning how to sell on eBay, share their insights on what types of items sell best on eBay in this chapter. They also offer tips on which eBay paid listing upgrades offer the best return—meaning a higher selling price—and which ones are money traps that should be avoided. In addition, the two share some straight talk about how to make sure serious bidders find your products in the vast universe that is eBay.

Joyner: I know you'll have a lot of insights and advice that you can offer, given how many different kinds of items you sell. Why don't we start by talking about how you two came to open an eBay drop-off store in Chicago.

Navarro: Amy and I met while working in retail. We had originally discussed opening an online clothing boutique together. Then we heard about this concept—I believe it was on National Public Radio (NPR)—of eBay drop-off stores. They were just in California at that point. We thought it was such a fabulous concept. We had extensive eBay knowledge through our personal lives. It was a low start-up cost business because all you needed was to pay the rent and buy a couple of computers and cameras to get started.

We decided to pursue this idea in late January of 2004, and we opened our doors six weeks later. It was a pretty quick process. We were really fortunate when we started. We got a ton of press. Business writers were really interested in the concept. They kind of considered it to be like a new dot-com at the time. We were featured in a full-page article on the front page of the *Chicago Tribune* business section. We were in Crain's. That kind of exposure just carried our business from the get-go.

PowerPointer

Be on the lookout for great business opportunities. Sometimes they pop up in the strangest places.

Joyner: So the publicity really helped in the beginning? And being the first to market in your particular area?

Navarro: Yes.

Joyner: This may be getting a little ahead of the game, but I wanted to ask you about your policies for accepting items for consignment and how those have evolved over the past two years. For example, an item must have a value of at least $50 before you'll accept it and post it on eBay. Have you always been so strict?

Mayer: We've always had the $50 threshold. But in the beginning, we definitely took more items that we weren't necessary confident would sell for $50. That's just because we were newer, and it was our way of getting our name out there. We're not necessarily more particular about what we take now, but our knowledge of eBay grows every day. We now know exactly what to take, because we understand what does and doesn't sell.

Navarro: It's a trial-and-error situation, as Amy mentioned. At first, we were taking anything that came in the door, and you lose money doing that. You have to think about the labor that's involved in posting items, packing them, and answering the questions about the merchandise. At the end of the day, if something sells for $20, we're losing a lot of money—especially if it's a 50-piece set of china that takes two hours to pack for shipment.

Joyner: Good point. When something like that comes in, like a set of china that seems like it could sell for a high price on eBay, how do you decide whether it's worth selling when it might take a lot of time to create the auction ad and package the product for shipment? That can be a real gray area for people selling on eBay. They don't take into account the cost of the time they're spending on the auction.

Navarro: Again, it's all experience and trial-and-error. You can search eBay's completed auctions until you're blue in the face. We've sold at least 15,000 items, so we've seen those 15,000 items come through our doors. That's the best experience you can get.

Power**Pointer**

Experience and trial-and-error are the best guides to figuring out how to price merchandise.

Joyner: People always ask me this—and I'm sure you get these questions a lot, too, in the classes you teach on eBay: What are the best categories? What are the most profitable? What items sell best?

Mayer: It's hard to say. Generally, musical instruments are great.

Navarro: Electronics.

Mayer: Collectibles. Sporting goods. We always say the golden rule is that it has to have a brand name attached to it.

As far as collectibles go, you could have this little porcelain statue that to you is priceless because your grandma gave it to you. But if it has no markings, it pretty much isn't going to sell. It's got no eBay value, versus something that's a Lladro or a Hummel.

Something we'd never turn down is anything Chanel or Louis Vuitton.

PowerPointer

Brand-name merchandise that buyers are familiar with almost always sells best.

Joyner: Do those designer items come in very often?

Mayer: Quite often, and they always sell for so much.

Joyner: Really?

Mayer: Yeah. We have a Chanel jacket up right now that's up to $830.

Joyner: Do you have any sense of what the retail price was?

Mayer: Probably $2,000. As far as clothing goes, Chanel has the highest resale value.

Joyner: I know you both have the experience working in retail and working in fashion. You mentioned two highly coveted brand-name designers—Chanel and Louis Vuitton. There are a lot of knockoffs of products from these brands on the market. How are you able to distinguish authentic merchandise from frauds, and how do you learn those skills?

Mayer: Again, it's experience. We've seen enough come through. We've done the research on what markings to look for in authentic items. There are certain markings on the zippers of some items. Louis Vuitton handbags have certain authenticity codes inside and they're always in specific places.

We've seen enough real items and enough fakes at this point to be extremely confident that we know what we're taking in. Of course, the fakes do get better every day, so you have to be up on what the actual companies are putting out.

Also, it helps to look at eBay's completed auctions to see designer items that sold for the highest prices. We're assuming that those are real. You can see what those sellers used to show authenticity.

Navarro: EBay has a tool now—"plogs" (buyers' guides created by other eBayers). If you search for Louis Vuitton on eBay, on the left-hand side of the screen, you'll see resource guides from people showing how to spot a fake. They have pictures of what fake handbags look like, what a fake serial number looks like versus the real one, and so forth.

EBay has worked really hard to give us the tools to make sure we know what's real and what's fake. I refer to those quite a bit.

Power**Pointer**

Check out eBay's "plogs" for tips from other sellers on various issues, such as how to spot fake merchandise.

Joyner: Do you sell a lot of clothing, given your background in retail?

Navarro: We do sell a lot of different items, but we actually have quite a niche in retail because we sell overstock for high-end retailers. About 80 percent of our business right now is selling overstock items for clothing stores. We sell for about 50 retailers across the country. At the end of the season when they don't want to move their stuff, we put it on eBay on their behalf.

Joyner: Do you charge these retailers the same commission rate you charge walk-in customers?

Mayer: It's 5 percent less.

Joyner: How did you develop these relationships with the retailers? One of the most frequent questions I hear from people wanting to sell on eBay is, "How do I find suppliers?"

Mayer: We were fortunate enough to have some existing relationships because of our backgrounds. A few stores actually approached us.

It worked out so well, we decided we should target other stores and tell them that we could consign their excess and out-of-season inventory on eBay. That is what we did, and we now have 50 retail clients.

Navarro: They're in all different parts of the country. They ship us their items at the end of the season.

Mayer: We were trying to become like a Bluefly on eBay.

Joyner: Are these big retailers that are providing you products to sell on eBay?

Mayer: They're all boutiques of different sizes. Some people send us 50 items, and others send us 5,000 items. It kind of runs the gamut.

Joyner: So some of these retailers may have more than one location? But many of them are small?

Navarro: Yes. It turns out that the smaller stores were a pretty under-served community in terms of options for their overstocks. Larger department stores have more options, but the smaller boutique owners were not being approached by anyone, really.

Joyner: Why would a retailer choose to consign merchandise to you to sell on eBay rather than just keeping it on the in-store sale rack indefinitely?

Mayer: There are a lot of reasons why it's more lucrative to sell through us on eBay.

If retailers have their stuff on sale for too long, it kind of starts to give customers a bad taste in their mouths. You want a good reputation. You want that sale stuff out of your store eventually. People just don't want to look at it anymore. And if you always have things on sale, people go straight to the sale racks and ignore the newer merchandise.

Joyner: What do you do with merchandise that you're unable to sell on eBay? What's your strategy for unloading it?

Navarro: With the retailers, we have a pretty good sell-through rate, definitely higher than the eBay average. It's over 60 percent. If we list an item more than one time for a retailer, it just hasn't sold for a low price, and there's no reserve, we may send the item back.

Fortunately, we rarely have to do that, because generally if we lower the price enough, it tends to sell.

For the individual clients, if they post something with no reserve at a very low starting bid and it doesn't sell, they have the opportunity to pick it up or we can donate it to charity. That doesn't happen often because we're generally able to pick out what can sell.

Joyner: What's your rule of thumb as far as pricing goes? I know particularly when you're selling on consignment, sometimes it's really hard to get those unfamiliar with eBay to agree to a low opening bid or to run an auction without a reserve.

Mayer: Some customers are like, "You're the expert. That's why I brought it to you." And they'll leave pricing to us.

Others are very stubborn, and they don't understand the auction process no matter how much you explain it. Ultimately it's their decision where to start the bidding, since they're paying for it.

People set way too high reserves sometimes, and we know an item is not going to sell. It's frustrating, but there's really nothing you can do.

Joyner: Do you use reserves very often?

Mayer: Yes. We have a basic and a premium package that people can choose from. The basic is free and starts with an opening bid of $19.99. The premium package is about $15, and with that you can set a bid of your choice and set a reserve.

Navarro: We encourage customers to use the basic option 90 percent of the time unless it's a really rare or unique item that we're not sure will sell.

Joyner: What is the reason for that? I really want to hear your philosophy on reserve-price auctions, which many successful eBay sellers don't like.

Mayer: We don't encourage reserves. Personally, if I'm bidding on something and I see there's a reserve, I don't want to deal with it. I'm just going to look for another option. Reserves discourage people from bidding at times.

Rather than doing a reserve of $200, just set the starting bid at $200.

Power**Pointer**

Instead of setting reserves on higher-priced merchandise, start the bidding at a higher dollar amount. Reserves can discourage people from placing a bid in the first place.

Navarro: I don't know necessarily when I would suggest a reserve versus a higher starting bid.

I might encourage a reserve over a higher starting bid if I felt that the item might not reach the seller's minimum price, and if they were willing to possibly sell it for less.

Let's say you had an auction with a starting bid of $19.99 and a reserve of $200. Say the bidding got up to $150, and the auction ended without selling. Then you have the opportunity to send a second chance offer to the high bidder.

If I felt that there was flexibility with the seller in what they would sell it for, I would probably recommend a reserve over a high starting bid in that case.

Joyner: I see. I guess you have to kind of know how to read people and practice a bit of psychology on your clients.

Mayer: That's the benefit of having retail experience when you open an eBay drop-off store.

Joyner: Talk more about that. How does your retail experience benefit you now that you're running an eBay drop-off company?

Navarro: I think that's what has made us successful over so many other eBay drop-off stores. Like Amy just said, some trading assistants and eBay drop-off store operators have only technical skills and no social skills.

It is such a personal thing to bring your item, such as your family heirloom, into the store to sell. We understand that. We treat that customer with the utmost respect and focus on being super-friendly because our business has been built through word of mouth.

Power**Pointer**

Customer service is a key differentiator for any business.

Mayer: We're providing a service that is very unfamiliar to a large percentage of the people who come to use it. It's really important that you have a strong retail background. It enables you to explain the process to customers, what the risks are for selling something with no reserve, and other things like that. You also know how to read people to see whether they're the kind of person that can handle the risk of a no-reserve auction.

Joyner: That reminds me of the movie *The 40-Year-Old Virgin*. One of the characters runs an eBay drop-off store, and there's a funny scene where she's trying to explain what it is she does for a living.

Navarro: It's still amazing to us how so many people don't even know about this concept, even now. I mean when we first opened, it was common.

Amy and I actually don't work at the stores anymore—we work out of our offices now. We did for two years, though, so we saw a lot of confused customers coming in. "Can I FedEx this item?" Or people wanting to buy things outright. And we're like, "No, we're an eBay drop-off store."

We've had people come in and try to sell some of the craziest stuff.

Joyner: I'm sure. What is the craziest thing that you can talk about that someone's tried to sell?

Navarro: We did sell, actually, a box of 30 brand-new catheters.

Mayer: Another was a hydraulic medical bed.

Navarro: We've sold buffalo skulls. People tried to sell live animals through us, which we obviously could not take. You name it—it's probably come in through our doors.

Joyner: I guess all of those things probably have an audience—hydraulic beds, buffalo skulls, the catheters. There's bound to be someone in the world looking to buy them.

Power**Pointer**

No matter what you sell, chances are there's a market for it on eBay. But it's always wise to do a little research before posting an item for sale.

Navarro: You're so right. All of the things we just mentioned sold pretty well as I recall.

Joyner: In those instances, do you just follow your gut instinct when deciding whether to accept an item for consignment? Is there a lot of data out there on eBay with regard to what buffalo skulls sell for, for example?

Mayer: There is, and that's one of the most surprising things. What we think might be very random we find there is an audience for once we start trying to research it on eBay. Maybe 10 or 100 have sold in the last 30 days, and you can't believe it.

Joyner: Since you set up shop, there has been a proliferation of eBay drop-off stores, some franchises and some locally owned. What sets yours apart from the others?

Mayer: I would say our focus on customer service. That's the number one thing that's most important to us in the stores.

Not only that, but we take great pride in each one of our auctions. We understand that the information contained in each auction—the pictures and the descriptions—is going to make or break the sale of the item no matter how great it is.

Navarro: There actually are two other eBay drop-off stores in the city of Chicago now. One just opened recently that's a franchise. The other is a local business. We've purchased items from them in the past to kind of see what they can provide. It was just a horrible experience. They wouldn't answer our e-mails for three or four days, and our items weren't shipped out for over a week, literally.

Joyner: That's not good.

Navarro: This has happened multiple times with this company. Mind you, it is in a much more prime location than we are, but we always seem to be doing a little bit better. I also think it's because we opened first, so we got all the word of mouth.

Joyner: In your case, customer service refers to how you treat the people who bring you merchandise to sell as well as to how you treat your customers on eBay. Do you have some benchmarks that you follow? If someone sends you a question about an item, how quickly is that going to be answered? How fast is an item going to be shipped once it has been paid for?

Mayer: We like to say that we'll answer any e-mail inquiry within 24 hours. Of course, if it comes in on a Saturday, it probably wouldn't be until Monday, but that's really the longest lag that you're going to see.

People can expect a quick response from us all around. They can expect their items to be posted quickly if they are a seller, and they can expect their items to be processed quickly if they're a buyer.

Power**Pointer**

Answer e-mail queries from potential buyers promptly—and always within 24 hours.

Joyner: When a consigner brings an item in, how quickly will it actually make it up on eBay?

Mayer: We say it will be up within seven business days, but it's rarely that long. It's normally about half of that.

Joyner: Some eBay sellers will say there are better days to sell certain items, or that you want your auctions to end on Sundays or Saturdays when people are home and on the Internet. Have you found any tricks of the trade like that?

Navarro: I really think that we've found that not to be true, with the exception of holidays. We don't allow auctions to end on holidays, just because people are so tied up with their own lives.

Joyner: That makes sense.

Navarro: But we have not found that ending an auction on a Sunday rather than a Tuesday really makes much difference at all. We do pay attention to time. We won't post something at 10:00 at night that would end at 11:00 at night on the East Coast.

We pay attention to time of day more than day of the week because we just haven't found the day to be that important.

Mayer: I think we would pay attention to time of day for another reason: customer service. We would want to make sure that, in the last moments of an auction, if somebody wanted to get a question answered, we could be there to answer that question, to make sure that if they want to bid, they could get their bid in.

If we were posting items that ended late at night when we weren't here in the office to answer those questions, that would probably impact not only the price, but also the service that we were providing to potential buyers because we wouldn't be available when they most needed the answers.

Power**Pointer**

Avoid having auctions end at times when you will not be in front of the computer. You want buyers to be able to e-mail their last-minute questions to you and get an answer right up to the close of the auction.

Joyner: In addition to running a successful eBay drop-off business, I know you also teach classes to people who are interested in buying and selling on eBay.

Are there any tips you can share, things that you've learned over these past couple of years that you think are really important for new sellers or sellers who want to take their eBay business to the next level?

Navarro: We definitely fill our two-hour classes with tips that we've learned. It's funny. The tips relate to both buyers and sellers. As a buyer, you should do X, Y, and Z to make sure that you get the best deal. And as a seller, you should do those same things to make sure your item gets seen by the most buyers and gets a lot of bids.

Mayer: I think people tend to overestimate the search function on eBay. Google and Yahoo! are so sophisticated, sometimes it seems like they can tell what you're trying to find even if you don't really search for it appropriately. On eBay, the search feature is not as sophisticated, nor as intuitive.

If you search for "pink sweater," you're only going to find current auctions with both "pink" and "sweater" in the title, spelled the exact way that you have chosen to spell it.

I think it's important as a buyer and a seller to keep that in mind and make sure, as a seller, that you have any and all of the words possible that somebody might be searching for, in addition to other ways to spell the item. For instance, Wedgwood china isn't spelled the way most people think that it would be. If we have an auction for that, we would probably spell it both ways.

Power**Pointer**

Understand that eBay's search function is limited compared to Yahoo! and Google. EBay relies strictly on keywords and won't help to steer buyers who aren't specific enough about what they are looking for in the right direction.

Joyner: Good example. My wedding china is Wedgwood, and even I'm not sure whether it's spelled with a second "e" or not.

Mayer: Right. You want to make sure that you catch both the people who do know and those who don't.

Joyner: Any other insights or tips you can share with our readers? Are there any listing enhancements that are definitely worth the extra cost?

Navarro: We use the eBay gallery for every auction. We think it's critical. Oftentimes people will not even look at the auctions that don't have a gallery listing, and that's just not something that we're willing to risk.

In general, we don't use many other listing enhancements. We rely on our titles and pricing in order to sell the items. There are a lot of potential add-ons on eBay, but every one costs money.

We just haven't seen a lot of return on most of them. That's not to say we wouldn't ever use them. If we had some dresses that retail for a few thousand dollars, that might be something that we'd feel needs to be in a featured auction. When we sell cars, we do featured auctions.

But the item price and likelihood of it selling at all has to be taken into account before we would ever increase our fees like that.

Power**Pointer**

Depending on what you sell, it may be beneficial to spend money on gallery listings or featured auctions. Just be certain your item is priced high enough, and that it is almost certain to sell based on your research, before shelling out dough for such advertising.

Joyner: I don't see a lot of sellers using it, but I've often questioned the benefit of using bold text in an auction's title.

Mayer: We used to offer bold in all of our auctions, and it's an incredibly expensive upgrade. It's a dollar. We did not find that there was much return on that at all, so that's not really something that we even offer now because we just feel that it's a waste.

There are some fees that are going to give you a far greater return. You have to balance that. A lot of people don't look at their auctions appropriately in terms of how to advertise their items. You need to use the appropriate advertising features available to you when you are marketing merchandise.

Power**Pointer**

Paying extra to use bold type in your listing is rarely worth it.

Joyner: Do you have any suggestions for writing headlines for eBay? Does the order of the words matter?

Navarro: We generally don't think the order has much to do with it. But you want to include the crucial information and keywords that people looking for a particular item are going to search for.

Joyner: Is eBay's vastness at all a detriment to sellers?

Mayer: That's a good question. I think that the vastness can be a detriment if a seller does not appropriately title their auction so that their auction eventually ends up in somebody's limited list of results once they go ahead and drill really far into the category they're looking at.

Joyner: How often do you utilize the "item specifics" feature within eBay that allows you to succinctly provide more information about an item's condition, size, and other features?

Navarro: I think that's extremely important, especially in women's clothing. There are so many items you're going to see. I think it's very important that you provide as much detail as possible so people can quickly search down and see only items that pertain to them.

Joyner: When someone comes into your store with items to sell, do you make them fill out a form? Do you interview them about the particular item? How do you get all the information that you need to write a good auction ad?

Mayer: They have a contract that they have to sign with their address and contact information. Then we do have a section that asks for a name and description of the item. We generally ask them to include information that we wouldn't automatically know about that item. If it's a piece of electronics equipment, we also ask for the status or condition. They have to stand by that because we can't test a lot of electronic items.

Joyner: How do you go about taking all that information and writing a compelling ad? How important are the words and photographs in an auction ad?

Navarro: Both are critically important. EBay would tell you that you should photograph your items as if there were no description, and you should describe your item as if there's no photograph.

People won't necessarily bid as much on your items if you don't provide a large amount of information.

PowerPointer

It's critical that your auction listing contains both compelling content and photographs. Still, you should write the content description as if there were no photographs, and vice versa.

Mayer: Here's something we have learned through experience: We used to write really flowery, romantic descriptions at the beginning, and people just don't want that. It's too much to read through. So we now make our descriptions pretty straight to the point: "You are bidding on a brand-new Chanel jacket in perfect condition." Then we'll write the style, size, color, and measurements. Then we'll include a paragraph about Chanel and about our company.

PowerPointer

Avoid using flowery and wordy descriptions. Go straight to the point when describing an item.

Joyner: So, eBay customers are not looking for the same kind of romantic copy they might appreciate when buying from a catalog?

Mayer: That's pretty much true for all items. If an item has a really cool story attached to it, like Joe Smith's grandmother got this when she was living in Nazi-occupied France, we might include that in the description. When there's some historic value attached to it, it's worth it to tell the story.

But we were saying things like "This jacket is great for wearing with denim and high heels and transfers into night," and just going on and on because of our retail background. We talked about what you could wear that piece with. We've had friends look at our items and say, "I don't want to read through that two-paragraph description. Just get to the point."

An additional reason brevity is so important is because people don't normally spend much time reading your listing. If you fail to get to the point and compel them right away to bid, they will move on to another merchant who is probably selling the exact same item, and perhaps even for less money. That's why you need to grab buyers right away with catchy, brief, and precise wording, along with compelling and clear photos.

8

Robert Walzer
Forklift Deals

First, eBay was tagged with a reputation for being *the* place to buy and sell knickknacks, along with everything from baseball cards and Beanie Babies to antiques and Bauer pottery. More recently, the web site, which has entered its second decade of operation, has become populated with merchants selling a variety of new, name-brand merchandise and is competing with the likes of Wal-Mart, Neiman Marcus, and every other retailer in between.

But there's another side to eBay of which many are unaware.

In addition to being immensely popular with consumers, the world's largest online flea mart is also a robust and thriving business-to-business marketplace. Company leaders are logging on to buy all kinds of supplies for their businesses—everything from pens and pencils to computers and heavy equipment.

Indeed, the vast business and industrial category is one of the most lucrative niches on the site, accounting for more than $1 billion in merchandise every year. The category includes such items as tractors and farm machinery, health-care supplies, medical instruments, building supplies, fax machines, office furniture, restaurant refrigerators, tools, and many other items that might be useful in businesses.

After a career in the aerospace industry that ended after he was laid off for the second time, online entrepreneur Robert Walzer found his niche selling products in the lucrative business and industrial category on eBay.

Walzer began his eBay venture in 2002. Initially he focused on offering surplus networking equipment and computers for companies in the Pacific Northwest. Then, Walzer found himself in the market for a forklift to ferry merchandise around his own warehouse. He was appalled by how much local dealers charged for the equipment and turned to the Internet in search of a better deal. Finding none, Walzer began contacting offshore forklift manufacturers, hoping he could locate someone willing to sell to him directly and cheaply. He found one such manufacturer and decided to buy a spare forklift, in addition to the one he planned to use in his own warehouse, just to see if he could resell it on eBay.

When the forklift sold—for a nice profit yet at a price that was still significantly below retail—Walzer began taking steps to expand his business. Today, his company, Forklift Deals, is the leading seller of new lift equipment, pallet stackers, powered pallet jacks, dock plates, forklifts, walkie stackers, wheel chocks, drum lifters, and other heavy-duty moving equipment on eBay.

The company, which operates under the eBay user ID forklift-deals, sells primarily to other businesses, and nearly every sale is a high-dollar one. Forklift Deals offers products ranging in price from $900 to $5,000, and the shipping charges alone often approach $500.

Despite those challenges, Forklift Deals is one of eBay's biggest players, with annual revenues in the millions. About half of the company's sales come directly from eBay; the rest are generated through the corporate web site at www.forkliftdeals.com. Many customers coming to the corporate site first bought from the company on eBay and have been spurred to make a repeat purchase based on that positive experience.

In this chapter, Walzer, who runs Forklift Deals with the help of his wife and five employees, shares his secrets for selling expensive industrial equipment—and business-to-business merchandise in general—on the Internet. He talks about how his company is able to undercut the prices of traditional retailers while also offering free freight on heavy, expensive-to-ship merchandise.

In addition, he offers tips for maximizing a product's exposure on eBay without paying inflated and unnecessary listing fees. Finally, Walzer reveals how he found overseas suppliers and how he manages those business relationships from afar.

Joyner: I'm really interested in talking to you because you sell goods in one of the most robust categories on eBay—business and industrial. How did you determine that there was a market for forklifts and similar industrial equipment online and on eBay in particular?

Walzer: There is certainly an interesting story behind that. Basically, my wife and I started our own business about four years ago, during a fairly significant recession in the Seattle area. After getting laid off from the aerospace industry twice in the same recession, I decided that somebody was trying to tell me something.

They say the definition of being insane is doing the same things and expecting different results, so I decided this was probably as good a time as any to actually go out and start my own business. I'd had people tell me for the last 20-some-odd years, "Rob, you should start your own business." I thought that if I could think up some great idea then maybe I would. But there were always people who would come back and say, "You know, the emphasis isn't on a great idea. It should be that you want to run your own business. You can figure out what that company does later."

We approached starting our business from this perspective: What are the real problems? What's the real environment that we're in? And what are we going to do about it? So, we sat down and went through a strategic planning process.

We decided we wanted to be in a services business rather than developing and manufacturing products. We decided that we wanted to be in the e-commerce world. But then we had to deal with the problem that even if we had some service for people to buy, why would customers want to buy it from us as opposed to somebody else?

A lot of people starting out in business go down the path of trying to be cheaper than the competition. That's not a bad strategy to begin with, in order to get in the door, but it doesn't really work in the long run.

Eventually we said, "What kind of problems are companies having and what can we do to fix them? How can we overcome the biggest problem, the biggest hurdle, in their businesses?"

We realized the biggest problem in getting someone's business is asking them for money. So we decided not to do that. We realized that during a recession a lot of businesses have excess inventory and supplies that they don't know how to deal with.

That's why we decided to start selling on consignment for technology companies. To win their business, we didn't have to ask them for any money because we were offering to solve a problem and actually offering to give them money back.

We've been doing this for about four years now. We focus on technology companies because that's my background. I know something about the dynamics of that world.

Joyner: But that's not the end of this story because at some point you branched out and began selling industrial equipment online as well.

Walzer: Two and a half years ago, as our business started to grow, we moved into a warehouse and started racking our inventory. We needed a forklift or a pallet packer. I started shopping for one and was appalled at the prices.

Being a guy who can't sleep and is always thinking, one night I decided, "Heck, why don't I just find a supplier in China and buy one direct?"

I found a supplier, got a quote, and instead of buying one, I bought two with the idea that I would keep one and sell the other.

A couple months later when the shipment arrived from China, we did just that and made a fair amount of money. So, I figured let's try it again. This time we bought four forklifts from China. A couple of months later, they arrived and we sold them.

Joyner: Did you sell them through eBay?

Walzer: Yes. Even today we only sell online. At that point we only sold them through eBay because we didn't have our own web site or any other channels to sell through.

Then we bought nine forklifts and sold those. We pretty much broke even. Now, we're buying about 20 forklifts at a time from China and making money on them.

Joyner: Are you a gambler? Do you go to Vegas a lot? Because it seems like you certainly took a gamble when you bought that first expensive forklift with the idea of reselling it on eBay.

Walzer: We've been to Vegas a couple of times, but I rarely gamble.

There is a huge difference in my mind between gambling and having confidence in yourself. I've always had a lot of confidence in myself. My way of looking at things is there are plenty of other people in the world who are importing all types of equipment. What makes them smarter or more capable than me?

As a matter of fact, I've always felt that by putting a little brainpower to a problem, I can probably solve it. Selling multithousand-dollar forklifts and material-moving equipment online doesn't seem to be particularly challenging to me.

Joyner: Obviously, you've figured out how to do it quite profitably.

Walzer: Exactly. About a year ago we started our own web site at www.forkliftdeals.com, and we now do about half our business there and the other half on eBay. We even have our own brand of equipment called Lift Science.

Joyner: Are you still working with the same manufacturer in China? Or have you struck deals with additional suppliers as you've grown?

Walzer: The problem with many industries, and material handling is one of the classics, is that they're locked up in a paradigm from 50 or 75 years ago in terms of selling, in that they sell through dealers and distributors. Most of the existing manufacturers have hooked up with dealer/distributor networks and it pretty much precludes them from having a real active presence on the Internet.

They might allow retailers to advertise their products online. But in terms of real Internet commerce, where all transactions are conducted online, they're not geared up for that sort of thing.

Turn the clock back 100 years to the early 1900s. If you wanted to buy a piece of equipment you had to physically go down to some local dealer or distributor. That's the same way these items are sold today. Most manufacturers of this type of equipment can't really take advantage of the Internet.

Power**Pointer**

Many manufacturers and buyers of industrial equipment are still doing business the old-fashioned way—by working through distributors, and not online. This creates challenges, as well as potential opportunities.

Joyner: Because they're so locked into the old way of doing business?

Walzer: Exactly. A lot of my customers are Internet-based businesses, so the Internet is the natural place they go to look for this type of equipment. They're comfortable buying there, and they're doing it during off hours, on the weekend, or on holidays. It's just a much more efficient, effective distribution platform.

Joyner: You're selling some pretty high-ticket items, not the sort of things people expect to see on eBay. Because of that, is yours a high-touch business? Do you have to have more communication with your customers? Do you have to respond to more customer questions?

Walzer: Yes and no. First of all, we probably do have to go a little further than some sellers in terms of making sure we have accurate descriptions of our products and things like that.

One of the nice things I've noticed as I've sold different products on eBay over the last several years is that you encounter more problems when selling to individual customers. Individuals have very fickle expectations in terms of their purchases, but business buyers tend to be, for the most part, much more reasonable.

Another advantage I have is I get to choose whom I do business with. Based on what someone says in an e-mail or on the telephone, it's not unusual for me to tell someone, "Don't buy from me. What you need is a local or national brand with a local distributor who can hold your hand and tell you that they love you." That's because that's what their expectation is. They need to go pay the price if they are looking for that kind of service.

If they are looking for a best friend or a golf buddy, it's not me. If they're looking for a good piece of equipment at the best price in the United States and they want to get it in a couple of days, then that's me.

Power**Pointer**

Business customers tend to be easier to deal with. They also have fewer fickle expectations than individuals tend to have.

Joyner: How do your prices compare with what someone would pay a local retailer for the same equipment?

Walzer: Typically we target prices to be about 50 to 75 percent of retail. Personally, if I can't get at least a 20 percent savings by buying something online, I might as well buy it locally. In that scenario, I can get the merchandise more quickly, I can get personalized service, and I can easily return the product if I decide that I don't like it two weeks from now.

I think about a 20 percent cost savings is about the minimum customers expect on the Internet. That's why we try to price things at 50 to 75 percent of retail. We adjust our prices sale by sale.

Power**Pointer**

When selling big-ticket business-to-business items, aim to charge about 20 percent less than local dealers do— including all shipping charges. Otherwise, you're probably not offering enough value for consumers to take the risk of buying from you sight unseen and having to wait for their purchase to be delivered.

Joyner: When you were talking about the cost savings that you offer over local dealers, does that include the shipping cost?

Walzer: Yes.

Joyner: When selling a heavy piece of equipment like a forklift, how difficult is it to keep freight costs low enough to make your product still attractive from a pricing standpoint?

Walzer: That's a huge issue. We're concerned not only with what it costs to ship items to our customers, but also the inbound freight expense, or what it costs to import the equipment from China.

When we started out, our inbound and outbound freight cost was pretty extreme. Now that our volumes are at a consistent level, freight costs have come down pretty dramatically. The other advantage is we ship out of multiple warehouses now. We operate warehouses in Dallas, Chicago, and Seattle.

Joyner: Do you own those warehouses? Or do you outsource the warehousing of your inventory?

Walzer: We outsource that. We actually handled all the warehousing ourselves for the first nine months, but that's the kind of business you want to leave to eager younger people.

Joyner: I know you sell different types of equipment. But give me an estimate of how much your average forklift weighs and how much a customer would have to pay to have one shipped.

Walzer: The average weight is about 1,600 pounds, roughly the size of two or three side-by-side refrigerators. Shipping for that typically runs $400 to $500.

Joyner: What's your average selling price?

Walzer: Our lowest-priced model is $899, and our highest-priced is $4,990.

Joyner: Do you sell at a fixed price on eBay?

Walzer: Not always. We sell in all formats. We sell through our eBay store, at a fixed price, and through auctions. We've sold forklifts for six cents.

Joyner: Yikes! Talk about selling at a loss. What does that feel like?

Walzer: It's kind of ironic. Most of the time, we do no-reserve auctions. When an item sells for some ridiculous amount of money like six cents it turns into being a nonpaying bidder about two-thirds of the time.

The bidder was probably someone who didn't want it, and was just sitting around playing and thinking, "I'll put a bid on this, but I'll never win it."

Then they win it and receive a congratulatory e-mail from us notifying them that it's the size of three side-by-side refrigerators and will cost $500 to ship.

As I said, two-thirds of the time those low bidders don't pay for the item. The other one-third of the time, when we end up selling the merchandise at a huge loss, I just look at it as part of doing business. It probably scares the crap out of my competition. I obviously don't sell a whole lot of them for six cents.

Joyner: How do you make the determination on how you list different products? What things do you put in your eBay store, versus what goes up for auction?

Walzer: The less expensive products that we have in quantity are listed in every format. Some of the higher-end items, which we don't sell in the same quantities, are typically put in our store and/or sold at a fixed price.

It's also based on supply and demand. That's why I said we change our prices all the time, sometimes on a daily basis. A guy called me yesterday and wanted to buy a certain model. I quoted him the price, and warned him it's all based on supply and demand. When he called, I had two of that model in stock, but warned, "If I sell one in the next five minutes and you call back, it's going to be more expensive." And that's just what happened.

When I have only one of something, and won't get another replacement in stock for six weeks or so, it's more valuable to me now than it was yesterday.

Joyner: Did that customer end up paying the higher price?

Walzer: Yes.

Power**Pointer**

Oftentimes, pricing must be based on supply and demand. That means you may wind up revising prices on a daily basis, depending on the item.

Joyner: I guess he realized you were still selling that piece of equipment for less than everyone else.

Walzer: Exactly. It all comes down to his time. He's done the research, he's talked to other people online, he's gone down to his local dealer and nearly passed out when he saw the price. He's also talked to a couple of other online merchants, but most didn't have the equipment in stock. Many other online sellers in my category are going to just order it from the factory, and it will be six or eight weeks before the merchandise arrives.

Joyner: Your business is different, however, because everything you have listed for sale on eBay and your site is in stock.

Walzer: I have it in stock or it will be in stock in a few days.

Joyner: That seems like a distinct competitive advantage you offer over other online sellers.

Walzer: Most online sellers of big equipment like this don't have stock.

PowerPointer

Having inventory in stock and ready to ship out right away gives you a competitive advantage, especially compared to other merchants who don't order merchandise until it has been sold.

Joyner: You said earlier that your sales are evenly distributed between eBay and your own web site. Are you trying to migrate more sales to your own site?

Walzer: You have to keep in mind these are two very different markets. EBay is almost considered to be a deal market, so things tend to sell at a lower price point. My own web site is a more mainstream market, and we tend to earn larger margins on items sold there. The question essentially is: Which market has more growth potential? I would say my own web site has more growth potential. We're already the number one seller of forklifts and similar industrial items on eBay. So, it's not like I can say there are a billion cameras sold on eBay and how can I capture a little bit more market share.

Joyner: Can you see a point where eBay is not a part of your sales strategy at all?

Walzer: I can't answer that other than to say that my gut feeling is that at some point several years down the road, eBay will represent a much smaller piece of my business. That's because I don't see eBay management doing anything to actively address business and industrial sellers. They seem to be more focused on selling more Beanie

Babies or whatever. Given that, I think eBay will be a much smaller piece of my business several years down the road.

Second, using my own web site, I'm in control of how I market. As soon as I get to the point where I can efficiently and effectively reach many of those same buyers without eBay, I may have less incentive to do business on the site. I would prefer that eBay executives stay focused on the core auction business and figure out how to increase the site's value to someone like me. I think that would be better all the way around in the long run.

Joyner: With a company like yours and the products that you are selling, is there a lot of potential for repeat business? What strategies do you use to market to those people who have already bought from you, be it through eBay or on your own web site?

Walzer: Every one of my products has my Web address painted on it, and it will be there for the next 30 years.

Power**Pointer**

> If you're selling large industrial items, be sure to put your Web address on the equipment so people will always know exactly where the product was purchased from.

Joyner: Have you done that from the beginning?

Walzer: Yes.

Joyner: So when your past customers need a forklift presumably you're the first company they think of?

Walzer: Yes, because they've seen www.forkliftdeals.com in front of their face for the last who knows how many years. Every time they use that piece of equipment, the URL is there.

These are capital goods. It's not like buying some consumable thing that disappears inside of days, weeks, or months. These things have a life span of maybe 20 to 30 years.

We also do Web advertising and have a mechanism for keeping in contact with people who have bought from us in the past.

Joyner: I gather you mine your auctions and keep a database of customers. Do you do any e-mail marketing to them?

Walzer: Not really. I haven't found that to be effective. People don't like getting e-mails. They get so many as it is.

Joyner: You didn't mention this specifically when you were talking about your web site versus eBay sales, but a lot of online merchants say it's so much more expensive to sell on eBay than through their own web sites because of the listing fees on eBay. When you are selling on eBay, what are some strategies you use to control your costs and minimize your listing fees?

Walzer: First of all, my own web site today is not necessarily less expensive to operate. It's less expensive in the sense I'm not paying ongoing sales commissions. But I do quite a bit of search engine pay-per-click advertising. That's not cheap.

One of the odd things about eBay—and members comment about this all the time—is they don't give any sort of volume discount for customers. So as I sell more and more, all my fees will add up, whereas on my own web site that's not the case. I have more of a fixed cost in terms of my own site.

On eBay I use a lot of second-chance offers. In the business and industrial category, there's a $20 minimum listing fee for a forklift. So even if I start bidding at a penny, it costs me 20 bucks to list it. If I do get a good sale price on it, I can extend second-chance offers to the runner-up bidders. If they decide to take the offer, I pay only a final valuation fee, which is pretty low.

Sometimes, I will pay to advertise an item on the eBay home page or feature an item. I may have paid $80 to list a single item, but if I sell a couple through second-chance offers, then that can save me a lot of money on the listing side.

Power**Pointer**

When offering merchandise with high initial listing fees (such as forklifts), use the second-chance offer option if you have additional quantities of the same item. This will save you from having to pay the high listing fee all over again.

Joyner: In the business and industrial category, where items tend to be more expensive, second-chance offers can really pay off as a way of controlling costs. This gives you a way to find qualified and motivated buyers, in much the same way that pay-per-click advertising does. It's an effective method for connecting with people who truly are interested in buying the product you're offering for sale.

Walzer: Right, and I get to decide whether to sell to them or not, unlike in an auction or a fixed price sale. I get to look at the potential buyer's feedback, their zip code, and things like that before even extending the second-chance offer to them.

For example, I look at their feedback and if they seem to have been a pain for other sellers to deal with, even if they've offered a good price, I might not give them a second chance because I don't need problem customers.

Joyner: Why would you look at someone's zip code before making a second-chance offer? Does it have to do with how close they are to one of your warehouses?

Walzer: Exactly. If I happen to know that I have a particular model in Seattle and the customer lives in Oregon, then maybe we can offer free shipping. But if he's in Florida, he probably doesn't get a second-chance offer.

Power**Pointer**

Check out bidders' feedback and other pertinent information before extending a second-chance offer to determine whether you really want to do business with them.

Joyner: In what instances do you offer free shipping?

Walzer: We offer it all the time because it just appeals to some people. The item doesn't necessarily cost them any less because usually the shipping cost is built into the sale price.

Joyner: Do you believe that someone today could do what you did a few years ago and discover a niche on eBay they could take as their own to build a business the size that yours is today?

Walzer: I don't see why not.

Joyner: I guess the question is: Are there still opportunities for more eBay success stories?

Walzer: Oh yes. It's like any other business. You have to determine what you are bringing to the marketplace, how you are going to compete, and how other companies are going to react.

It's probably a little more difficult today to build a successful eBay business than it was when I started because eBay has cranked up its fees over the years. So you're paying more money to list, and it's also more difficult to grow a successful eBay business. But it's certainly possible.

Joyner: Talk to me a little bit, if you will, about the challenges of dealing with a supplier overseas and breaking into that market. As you mentioned earlier, there are a lot of companies importing products from China. But it can be difficult to establish lucrative importer-exporter relationships. Are there any lessons you care to share about working with overseas vendors? Was it difficult to find a Chinese manufacturer that was willing to sell its products to you?

Walzer: For me it wasn't, but I can imagine it would be very difficult for most people—not necessarily difficult in the sense that finding a cure for cancer is hard. But it's hard because it makes their brain hurt. They don't know where to start. They don't know what to do. They're afraid of making mistakes, afraid of doing the wrong thing. But that's true whenever you're starting your own business, no matter what it is.

Joyner: How often do you travel to China?

Walzer: Every couple of months.

Joyner: Does buying from oversees suppliers require you to take an active role in the manufacturing process and the oversight of it?

Walzer: Is it required? No. Should you be? Yes. Those are two different things.

Joyner: I wrote a book a few years ago with Maxine Clark, founder and chief executive officer of Build-A-Bear Workshop. Her company buys a lot of products from overseas. Maxine is constantly traveling back and forth between the United States and Asia, and is in frequent communication with her suppliers. She stressed to me the importance of finding vendors that you can trust, but that's not to say you leave everything in their hands. You still have to manage the relationship.

Walzer: I think that's very true.

When beginning the process of finding an overseas supplier to work with, proper due diligence is of the essence. Ideally, try to visit the supplier in person, like Walzer and Maxine Clark have done. At the very least, you need to talk to others doing business with the suppliers to make sure they are reputable and reliable. Chances are, regardless of what you sell, you'll be dealing with an international supplier of some sort, because that's clearly the trend these days.

9

Nir Hollander

Gem Stone King

In the online jewelry business, especially on eBay, a company's reputation can mean the difference between success and failure. Ever-cautious online shoppers are even more careful when spending big money on expensive purchases, such as diamond engagement rings and other sparkling baubles.

In terms of reputation, Gem Stone King has a head start on its competition. Not only is the Manhattan-based company a pioneer in the fine jewelry category on eBay, but Gem Stone King also has a long and respectable history in the diamond industry.

Fine jewelry has been the company's focus for four generations.

Gem Stone King was founded in 1903 by Nir Hollander's great grandfather, who established a diamond-cutting factory in Antwerp, Belgium. For more than a century, Hollander's family has worked with diamonds and other gemstones, transforming raw, uncut stones into beautiful pieces of jewelry. His father, Charlie, is a well-respected diamond manufacturer and wholesaler, operating out of the famed diamond district in New York City.

Nir Hollander joined the family business in 1999, but grudgingly.

He had no interest in following in the professional footsteps of his father, grandfather, or great grandfather. But he did have enough sense to recognize a good business opportunity when he saw it, and began efforts to move the family business online, specifically to eBay.

As he witnessed other entrepreneurs not just succeeding but thriving on eBay, Hollander began selling fine jewelry through the site as well, marketing his family's products directly to consumers instead of through wholesale channels for the first time. That turned out to be a stroke of genius, both for Gem Stone King and for its customers. EBay, with its low overhead, offered a comfortable profit margin. Customers, who were now paying wholesale instead of retail prices for their diamonds and jewelry, felt like they were getting a bargain. And they were.

During its eight years on eBay, Gem Stone King, selling under the user ID gemstoneking, has grown into a Titanium PowerSeller with annual sales of more than $1.8 million. What's more, the company has received more than 25,000 positive feedbacks from customers—and nary a negative—thanks to its emphasis on honesty, transparency, and stellar customer service.

In addition to selling its own jewelry on eBay, Gem Stone King now functions as a trading assistant for other jewelry manufacturers and retailers wanting to expand their business to the Internet but lacking the expertise or infrastructure to do so. Those trading assistant relationships benefit Gem Stone King, as well as its partners, Hollander says. Obviously, there is a financial benefit in the commissions Gem Stone King earns for selling for other jewelers, but the rewards the company reaps extend much further than that. By selling for these other businesses, Gem Stone King is able to offer its customers more merchandise and variety without incurring any additional inventory costs. That strategy has enabled the company to continue to grow even as more online jewelry merchants have entered the marketplace.

In the following pages, Nir Hollander discusses how his traditional family business transitioned into an eBay powerhouse. His story provides a concrete example of how honesty can really pay off, in terms of both repeat business and a company's continued profitability. Hollander also offers his insights on what scrupulous eBay sellers can do to combat fraud on the site and preserve the online marketplace for years to come.

Joyner: I know you've been selling on eBay for a long time. Tell me how Gem Stone King evolved from a wholesale jeweler to one of the Web's most successful online retailers.

Hollander: My father is a diamond wholesaler. I'm the fourth generation in the business. But I wasn't really very interested in the jewelry or diamond business after college. I was really thinking more about a career in tourism and other things. I came to New York to do my MBA. When I got here, I became more business-oriented and saw the opportunity to take our family business online.

My father did business the old-fashioned way, which was not so attractive to me. By contrast, the online business model looked very compelling.

Joyner: When you joined Gem Stone King, was the company selling online at all, or just out of the diamond district in New York?

Hollander: My father has been a wholesaler for a long time in this business and we had wholesale customers all over the world—New York, Belgium, Israel, Australia, and Japan.

I wanted to be dedicated to the online part. I wasn't interested in all of the other aspects of the business. It was the concept of e-commerce— not jewelry—that was so attractive to me.

In the beginning, the idea was to sell our jewelry directly to consumers instead of selling it to retailers and others in the trade. Like any other eBayer, we started putting items up for auction on eBay and selling them. This is how we grew our business.

Joyner: How have you been able to convince consumers to spend huge amounts of money with you on eBay? After all, jewelry is an expensive and often personal purchase, and some might not feel comfortable buying it online.

Hollander: I can definitely tell you that we have learned a lot. Unfortunately, there are a lot of jewelry sellers playing all kinds of games on eBay. They're doing things like using shill bidding to drive up their prices and cheating consumers. But we don't operate that way. It's just the way we are.

We are very straight, and that makes it very tough for us because there are other sellers not playing fair. But I think we have a lot of repeat customers because people appreciate our honesty. We are different.

Power**Pointer**

> When selling a high-priced item like jewelry, understand that the occasional fraudulent competitor comes with the territory. Stand out from the competition by always being straightforward and honest in all of your dealings with buyers.

Joyner: So, you're saying that in the jewelry category there are some unscrupulous sellers who will place fake bids on their own items to drive up the price? And that they may be passing off lower-quality merchandise as authentic?

Hollander: The jewelry category is a mess. I'm sure every category has its own problems, but jewelry is a big, big mess. The reason is because it's a very difficult category to police unless you have expertise in the jewelry business.

It's tough for eBay's Trust and Security officials or consumers to look at an auction ad and determine whether the asking price is reasonable and if the item is what it's purported to be.

For example, someone can't be selling a one-carat, H-color, SI1 diamond for $1,000. That price is just too low.

As a wholesaler, I can look at an item and tell you if a price makes sense. If I can buy and sell an item to the trade for more than the eBay asking price, I know there's something dishonest going on. There's no reason for a wholesaler to sell an item to an end consumer for less than they could sell it to a retailer. This means that the item is clearly not what it is advertised to be. That is just one kind of fraud, where people misrepresent their items.

Joyner: What can be or is being done to rein in this fraud on eBay?

Hollander: We've created a dialogue with eBay and the other reputable jewelry sellers to address fraud. EBay made some rules. For example, you cannot put cubic zirconia (CZ) and man-made diamonds in the diamond categories.

Even though we have a good reputation and so much feedback, we always say "natural diamond" or "we only sell natural diamonds" in our descriptions. Even with that, we still get a lot of e-mails asking, "Is it natural?"

Joyner: Did you anticipate that fraud would be such a big issue when you first started selling on eBay? Or maybe the better question is, what made you think that people would be willing to buy expensive jewelry items, and specifically diamonds, from Gem Stone King on eBay?

Hollander: There are a lot of reasons.

One, e-commerce in general is something that is increasing every day. There is a huge potential market. Today, online jewelry sales, for example, are a small percentage of total jewelry sales, though that number is increasing.

I remember when I started and told wholesalers that I was selling online. They were very skeptical. "No, you cannot sell online," they said. Today, a lot of wholesalers are looking online. The business is really attractive. It's something they're thinking about much more seriously today.

Not everybody can go to 47th Street in New York to buy jewelry. Online, we have customers all over the world.

As for our success, I give better customer service and better prices than retailers, and being so transparent, that helps our sales. There are a lot of repeat customers. People come back again and again.

Repeat business could be the lifeblood of your company.

Joyner: I know from my own experience, when my husband bought my engagement ring, he bought it from a very reputable local jewelry store, because he wanted someone who would spend time with him and help educate him. Now he feels like he has a relationship with that store. He goes back there to buy anniversary gifts and the like. And he trusts them. Do you feel like you are able to do that same sort of thing with your online customers and that they feel that way about your company?

Hollander: Obviously, at the end of the day, a lot of people would say, "I need to touch or see my jewelry before I buy it." Then there is the trust. But I believe in online selling. I know for a fact that we can give better prices because we are the ones selling jewelry to the retailers. The same items are much more expensive at a retailer than from a wholesaler like us.

A lot of customers are willing to spend extra money to feel the assurance, to touch the item, and I totally understand it. On the other hand, there are a lot of people today—and the numbers are growing—who enjoy the ease of shopping online. They trust online merchants like me.

A second benefit to shopping online is the variety. When you go to a local jeweler, there's a limit to how many items he can show you. On top of this is customer service. It's true that a local jeweler you trust will give you good customer service, but he cannot show you a list of 10 people who were happy like we do with our eBay feedback. You don't know if somebody just left the door a few minutes ago and was unhappy with something. When someone buys from us on eBay, they see 25,000 people who were happy.

Power**Pointer**

Positive feedback serves as a potent customer referral mechanism.

Joyner: And they actually get to read those consumer comments in the eBay feedback forum.

Hollander: Exactly.

On top of this, we offer a full refund. It's really a win-win situation. We want you to be happy. The idea is not to make one sale. We don't want to make one sale and that's all. We know that repeat customers are our core business. We want them to come again and again.

We are very dedicated. I am very committed to online sales and to customer service. I work very hard on the description of the item to make sure a piece of jewelry is accurately depicted online.

Joyner: How difficult is it to accurately depict diamonds and other jewelry on a computer screen so that customers can have the confidence to bid and won't be disappointed in the item after the purchase? In other words, how do you show me the sparkle on the screen?

Hollander: It's very, very tough. A lot of diamonds look the same. If you go to all the biggest online jewelry and diamond sites, everything is a stock picture. There's no real picture of the actual item you're buying. It's all a representative sample.

But it's a different audience on eBay.

Joyner: Buyers want the picture of the precise item that they are bidding on?

Hollander: Exactly.

Even though I have the real description and the real picture and after all the e-mails, I totally understand that customers sometimes may not be satisfied with an item after they purchase it. That's why we have a full refund policy regardless of anything.

Somebody bought an item yesterday for $6,000. Yes, she can return it if she wants. I don't think she will because the item is so nice and attractive. Because our photographs and description are correct and very detailed, most of the time we don't get returns. But we do have some. It's part of online business.

Power**Pointer**

One of the most effective ways to instill confidence in buyers is to offer a full refund if they are unsatisfied for any reason.

Joyner: How do you protect yourself against fraud?

Hollander: That's a good question. A lot of people think as a buyer that they need to protect themselves from fraud. But to be honest, I can say as a big seller, we have been targeted from all over by buyers who are trying to send us false credit cards and false information.

Through experience, we've learned when to ship, when to accept the payment, and what kind of payment to accept.

I will tell you that we have been burned. It was a learning curve. We learned a lot by trial and error.

Joyner: How have you been burned?

Hollander: Let's say somebody pays with a credit card. Everything seems okay, so you ship the item once you have the money in your account. A month later, the credit card is reported stolen and the company reverses the charges. You have no money and the item is gone. It happens a lot if you're not careful about verifying that the person using the credit card is really the owner of that card.

Joyner: You've spoken a lot about transparency to the consumer. I'm hoping you can elaborate a little bit more on that. What product disclosures are important in your category or any category?

Hollander: When I say transparency, obviously I mean the description. The same way we grade a diamond in the trade, selling to our friends in the trade, that's the same way that we'll grade it to the consumer. We'll show them the same estimate, picture, description, and certification whether we're selling to a wholesale customer or someone on eBay.

Obviously consumers don't understand as much as we do about jewelry. So, a lot of fraudulent sellers will use this to their benefit and use false authenticity or appraisal certificates that aren't worth the paper itself.

When I say transparency, it means having a toll-free phone number that customers can call with questions. It means answering all e-mails. It means writing accurate descriptions. In the case of eBay, feedback is so important. If any seller has significant feedback, I think it's a proof of honesty.

Joyner: When you've got a feedback score of more than 25,000, that has to mean something to bidders.

Hollander: Exactly. It means that you're working very hard to satisfy your customers and do all the things I enumerated before. You cannot achieve success without doing that because people are so picky. If you do something even a little bit wrong, they will let you know.

This transparency, this feedback system, along with the generous refund policy creates amazing assurance for the customer.

Joyner: As a seller, you definitely want that positive feedback. That's the Holy Grail of eBay, and it seems to be crucial to the success of most PowerSellers. How, then, do you deal with negative feedback from customers?

Hollander: I try to reply and show customers what really happened from my perspective. If it's something that we can resolve through mutual arbitration, I'll do it.

Power**Pointer**

Don't ignore customers who write to you with complaints or provide negative feedback. Share your side of the story, and try to come to a mutual compromise so you both end up happy. You may be able to convince the customer to withdraw their negative feedback.

Joyner: I gather it's important for you to find out the reason behind that negative feedback.

Hollander: Always. I want to see what I did and learn what I should change and do differently next time.

Joyner: Do you get many calls from eBay customers asking questions about an item before they bid?

Hollander: I can say for a fact that the amount of customer service required per item on eBay is much higher compared to sales through Amazon or our web site. EBay buyers are much more demanding and require a lot more customer service. This is something that takes a lot of your time.

I basically don't believe in the idea that people should have to call you before making a purchase. I do list a phone number with all my auctions. If it's an expensive and difficult item to sell, I want buyers to be able to ask all the questions they need to in order to really feel assured and secure when they buy the item. But I really believe that in a pure online environment, all of the pertinent information needs to be in the auction listing itself so buyers can make an informed decision.

Joyner: Still, you include your phone number with every auction so that if people have a question, they can call and get that question answered.

Hollander: Right. I believe in full transparency. I put the phone number in because I want them to call if they feel they need to call.

PowerPointer

Full transparency is crucial. Make sure customers can get in touch with you in a variety of ways, including e-mail and telephone.

Joyner: What's your approach to pricing merchandise? It seems like you use a variety of techniques, including 99-cent opening bids and Buy It Now pricing.

Hollander: We have run a lot of auctions with low opening bids, and most closed at prices we could live with. Today, however, the auction prices on jewelry have really gone down. Customers need to be very careful when they see a low-starting-bid auction on a medium- to high-end item because that's very risky for the seller.

Joyner: I trust that to protect your profit margins, you're much more likely now to set a Buy It Now price, or sell at a fixed price through your eBay store, than to put expensive items up for bid at 99 cents. But by doing this, do you miss out on the competitive draw of auctions and the natural consumer desire to haggle for a good deal?

Hollander: When eBay came up with the "Make Offer" feature, we in-corporated that into our business. Haggling is something that is com-mon in the wholesale trade. On eBay, we also are able to accept, decline, or counter an offer that is being given by our customer. You can make up to three offers and counteroffers per customer, so it's a dynamic feature.

Joyner: I'm not sure that many buyers and sellers are familiar with the Make Offer or Best Offer option on eBay. In essence, a seller sets a Buy It Now price, which a customer could agree to pay. But under these options, the customer can also begin a price negotiation by making a lower offer.

Hollander: We don't always allow customers to make an offer. Some-times I just put in the very best price, the minimum price I'm willing to accept, and don't entertain any offers. But for a lot of items, yes, we will take offers.

Joyner: I'm looking at a ring you're selling right now with a Buy It Now price of $735. But you're also giving shoppers the opportunity to make an offer. Why would anyone buy the ring for $735 when they could make an offer and get it for less?

Power**Pointer**

If you have any flexibility with high-priced items, consider using eBay's "Make Offer" or "Best Offer" features, which give buyers the upper hand in haggling.

Hollander: A lot of people don't understand the concept, and they have wishful thinking. They think that if I put a ring worth $10,000 on eBay, I'll take their offer of $10. Obviously there are those who don't understand the concept.

Then you have a lot of serious people who make an offer that is a small percentage below your asking price. It's at that point the negotiation starts. It's interactive. The bidder still thinks that they win an item for a better price, which is true, by the way.

There are sellers who will say this is not a good practice. All over the world, though, people are used to bargaining and negotiating when somebody gives them a price. Here in America, we are spoiled. You go to the store—that's the price you pay.

Joyner: Right. But the Make Offer feature gives consumers some control over what they pay, just as an auction does. It creates some of that back-and-forth negotiation that some people really enjoy, like when you go to buy a car or haggle over prices at an antique store or a flea market.

Hollander: For some items—a diamond solitaire, for example—there really is a market price. It's a commodity. And there's no reason in the world to sell it below this price. So, we probably wouldn't entertain offers on items like that. But maybe my father and I manufactured a particular piece of jewelry that we thought was going to be a really good seller. But you know what? It's been sitting there a year, and it's not moving. Why not allow somebody to make me an offer? In this case, entertaining an offer makes a lot of sense.

Joyner: How often do you refuse offers?

Hollander: Today, somebody put in an offer for $2,000 on an item that she really wanted. I declined. I gave her a counteroffer. She sent me an e-mail saying she really wanted it for her anniversary. The note was really touching, but I cannot sell below cost. I told her that. I gave her a ridiculous price, and it's the best price in the world. Nobody can beat this price, but she wants to pay less. Maybe that's her budget, but I just cannot sell her the jewelry for her price. So it happens quite a bit when people are unrealistic.

Joyner: When you accept an offer from someone, how are your eBay fees calculated? Is eBay's fee based on your initial asking price or the final price of the item?

Hollander: The final-value fee.

Joyner: But your initial insertion fee is based on the initial asking price? That means you're paying a little bit higher fee when you choose to entertain offers.

Hollander: Yeah, that's true, but in my case, my average selling price is about $500. It used to be lower. I'm already paying a high insertion fee regardless. It averages around $5.

Joyner: What's the advantage of selling some items through eBay auctions and others through your eBay store?

Hollander: It allows us to diversify. Even though we don't always get the best price for auctions because you have no control over the bidders, we still do them. Some people are getting a really good bargain at the end of the day. But auctions are definitely a loss leader. They bring traffic to your store.

Joyner: So, you believe in using all the different listing methods available to you as a way of advertising your products on eBay and achieving the best possible sell-through rate and the highest possible profits?

Hollander: Yes. I have a lot of expenses as a serious, dedicated business. I have employees. I have office space. I need to cover these expenses.

Joyner: How important are other channels to you beyond eBay? Do you sell a lot through your own web site and as an affiliate of Amazon.com? How have you diversified these past six years?

Power**Pointer**

While there's no denying the huge audience available to you through eBay, be on the lookout for other sales channels, including Amazon.com and your own web site.

Hollander: Right now, not enough. It's something we are targeting this year, and we are now doing all kinds of things to increase our off-eBay business.

Obviously we have the wholesale business, and we have some off-eBay business, but eBay is still a very big part of our online business, and we want to continue to increase it if we can.

We still believe in eBay. We like eBay, even though it's tough and difficult at times. We like the whole concept of eBay. EBay is something that is part of my life. On the other hand, I'm also thinking of other channels.

Joyner: Readers wanting to learn more about how to grow their business through various other channels beyond eBay should check out my book *The Online Millionaire*, which discusses the whole concept of multichannel online marketing. Given that you have such a high percentage of repeat business on eBay, how are you cultivating that? Are you marketing directly to people who've bought from you before?

Hollander: Sure. We e-mail them with all kinds of messages. Once a customer is yours, and you have his e-mail and his permission to market to him, you can send him coupons, deals, and other offers.

Power**Pointer**

Once you have a customer's permission, stay in regular communication by sending out periodic e-mail messages with coupons, deals, and other offers.

Joyner: In that way, you must be bringing in some repeat business to your web site and other channels instead of to eBay. Is that your goal, to have people buy from you on your own web site instead of on eBay so you avoid paying the auction site's transaction fees?

Hollander: I have no problem with funneling buyers to eBay. A lot of sellers will tell you the idea of marketing is to bring people to your off-eBay site. But in my opinion, in my stage of the business, I just want them to buy. Whatever and wherever they buy, it is good. Whatever they feel comfortable with, that's good for me.

Joyner: I guess part of the reason they're coming back to you on eBay is that they already feel comfortable buying from you there.

Hollander: They're eBay shoppers, at the end of the day. They like the concept of making an offer, or bidding, or using PayPal. They have an account on eBay. They trust feedback.

Joyner: You're very active with PeSA, the Professional eBay Sellers Alliance. How has that been important to your business? What do you think sellers gain from being a member of a group like PeSA, or what I like to call The eBay Billionaires' Club?

Power**Pointer**

Network with other successful eBay sellers so you can share and benefit from mutual best practices.

Hollander: We are all trying to leverage our networking and know-how to increase our business, and not only on eBay.

It's networking at the end of the day. For example, in 2006, we met in San Francisco with representatives of Amazon, Yahoo!, eBay, and Google.

It was a lot of experience in one room—all the big sellers in different categories who really know a lot of things. It was the best networking ever.

Joyner: I'm always surprised at how willing these big sellers are to share their knowledge and expertise with others. It's a competitive field, but most PowerSellers are forthcoming when it comes to talking about their businesses and sharing tips for selling on eBay.

Hollander: Yes. We are sharing things that can help all of us.

As Hollander can attest, working together and sharing best practices really benefit everyone. Don't hesitate to call on other merchants as you grow your online business to share your respective secrets of success. You're all bound to benefit from the dialogue.

10

Jim Orcholski

J&T Coins

Jim Orcholski has been a coin collector ever since he was a kid. Although work, marriage, children, and all of the other stuff life brings took him out of the hobby for a while, he turned to eBay in 2001 hoping to revive his faltering coin collection.

Orcholski began using the auction site as a trading platform, both buying new coins and selling off things that he didn't want anymore. About a year into this, Orcholski reached a turning point after realizing coin dealers, not just other collectors, were buying from him. At that point, Orcholski made a decision to turn the corner from hobbyist to professional eBay seller.

"It grew to much more than I ever thought it would be, to be honest," admits Orcholski, whose professional background is in finance. These days, he's the proprietor of J&T Coins, an Internet-based business that deals in collectible coins. The company originated on eBay, and Orcholski still sells about $40,000 to $50,000 in merchandise on the auction site every month. But in the past five years, J&T Coins has expanded into other online and offline sales channels, specifically the wholesale dealer-to-dealer market and a stand-alone web site at www.jtcoins.com. EBay, which was once 90 percent of the company's business, now accounts for about a third of J&T Coins' annual revenues of nearly $2 million.

Orcholski, who lives in Oconomowoc, Wisconsin, about 40 miles west of Milwaukee, began his company with only a $250 investment. But he has constantly reinvested profits back into the business to fuel growth. He routinely buys coins in huge volume, usually spending a minimum of $25,000 on each order with his wholesale suppliers.

J&T Coins survives on repeat business, which is somewhat unusual for an eBay merchant.

Orcholski limits his eBay stock to mostly gold and silver coins, priced anywhere from $20 to $2,300. Buyers have the choice of bidding on items at auction or buying them at a fixed price from the J&T Coins eBay store. While Orcholski has booked several $10,000 orders, the company's average sale on eBay is $54, including shipping charges. Interestingly enough, about two-thirds of customers who bid on merchandise from J&T Coins check out the company's auctions every day.

Collectible coins, by their very nature, tend to attract repeat buyers, Orcholski says. But that's only part of the reason he has such a high return-visit rate on eBay. Here's the other side of the coin: Orcholski markets aggressively to past buyers, and he provides a level of customer service that is aimed at winning customers for life.

"If you want to be successful on eBay, you have to give good service," he insists. "You have to be fair to a fault. We try to correct our mistakes. If a customer has to return something, we reimburse for shipping, even if they only changed their mind. We're trying to build a long-term relationship with our customers."

In the following pages, Orcholski talks about strategies other eBay sellers can employ to increase their repeat business on the site. He rails against fraud and shares his secrets for fighting spammers, phishers, unscrupulous buyers, and other malicious people who are defiling the eBay marketplace. He also discusses the importance of diversifying into other online channels beyond eBay.

Joyner: At this point, do you collect coins at all yourself?

Orcholski: Not anymore. Everything I have is for sale now.

Joyner: I hear that same type of thing from a lot of people who have turned what was once a hobby into a business. Would it be a conflict of interest to try to be a collector and a seller of the same merchandise?

Orcholski: I think it would be.

Joyner: For someone who is not familiar with coin collecting, are there certain things that you specialize in?

Orcholski: I specialize in bullion, which is gold, silver, platinum, and palladium. I specialize mostly in foreign, modern coins—modern being the twentieth and twenty-first centuries.

Joyner: Is there a big market for recently minted coins?

Orcholski: Sure, because the series are issued on a yearly basis. A good example is the Chinese panda. The Chinese mint gold panda coins every year. They started doing them in 1982, and it has continued every year since. People buying since 1982 continue to buy the new coins every year, and you get new buyers in as well. By new buyers, I mean people who are new to the hobby of collecting. We also sell to investors.

Joyner: Are those new to the hobby looking to buy coins from all the years they missed?

Orcholski: The backdated coins can be very expensive because there is a limited availability. It is therefore more economical to start with the current years because those are normally the least expensive. We sell current and backdated coins.

Joyner: How much have you had to educate yourself about this hobby in your pursuit to become a professional seller on eBay?

Orcholski: Education is continuous. We're always learning new things. There are a lot of coins in the world and you can't know everything. It's just not possible. So, people tend to specialize. Even with what I specialize in, you're continuously learning. You learn something new every day. I know more than I did five years ago.

Power**Pointer**

No matter what you sell or what industry you're in, you will constantly be learning new things that can help make your business more streamlined and profitable.

Joyner: I'm sure the marketplace has changed a lot in five years.

Orcholski: It changes continually. It changes day to day. Certain items can be really popular one day, week, or month and before you know it they're not and prices just plummet. The market is always changing.

Part of the reason is that the prices of coins are based, in part, on the spot price of the metal at that time. And the spot price of the metal changes continuously. It's traded like a stock, so your pricing is always changing.

Joyner: Given those fluctuations, how do you price on eBay?

Orcholski: You have to buy right. The larger quantity you can buy, the better wholesale pricing you get.

Power**Pointer**

In general, the larger the quantity of merchandise you buy, the better price you will pay.

Joyner: Is fraud a big concern in your category?

Orcholski: It's a huge concern. There's a lot of concern with fake Chinese silver panda coins coming over from China, along with fake U.S. trade dollars or Morgan dollars. These are silver dollars that were used from 1921 and before, and some of them are quite expensive. There are a lot of fake coins of this nature on eBay right now.

Joyner: How does that affect you as a legitimate seller?

Orcholski: Sometimes it drives people away from eBay because they get burned and don't come back. Sometimes it brings buyers to us because of our positive feedback. Or maybe they've dealt with us before and know we're aboveboard. I've had people buy a small item and once they get it, they might buy more.

We do about two-thirds repeat business every month on eBay. They call it a return ratio. Our return ratio is about 3.25 to 1. We have one of the higher return ratios on eBay.

Joyner: A lot of people say eBay is not a place to get return business. I guess if you're selling something like a DVD it probably isn't. But in a collectible category such as yours, that doesn't have to be the case. What things are you doing in order to achieve a high return customer ratio?

Orcholski: It takes a while to build collections, so naturally buyers are going to come to us to round out their collections.

For example, the Australians put out a series of coins based on the Chinese lunar cycle. It started in 1996, and the last year is 2007. People will possibly want to collect the whole series. If you're a collector and you have only so much money to play with every month, it may take you a while to do that. What we sell is really not a necessity; it's a collectible. And people are using disposable income to buy it. A lot of people have only so much disposable income each month. They buy from us the first time and hopefully they'll come back until they complete the set they want to buy. Maybe they'll also buy something else along the way.

Joyner: Are your offerings mostly sold at a fixed price on eBay?

Orcholski: No, most of our merchandise is sold through auctions. We start them at 99 cents.

Joyner: What are your results with that?

Orcholski: We probably lose money on maybe 20 percent of our items.

Joyner: Why keep pricing that way then?

Orcholski: You want to draw people in to buy other things. They become familiar with you and they go to your web site or buy things out of your eBay store, and hopefully they'll come back and bid on other things, which will drive up the price.

PowerPointer

Starting bids at a low price point is a great way to draw buyers in.

Joyner: But obviously some things will sell for 99 cents, and lose you money in the process.

Orcholski: When I say we lose money, it's maybe two or three dollars. It's not a great deal per item, but it adds up over the course of a year. If you know what you're doing, you earn enough on the other items to make it still worthwhile to remain in business on the marketplace.

Joyner: Have you been affected at all by the listing fee increases in eBay stores?

Orcholski: When eBay raises its prices, we raise our prices. Have our sales decreased because of that? Yes, but that's the way it goes.

Joyner: What you're saying is that 99-cent auctions are a way to capture the attention of bidders. And if you lose money because of that pricing strategy, you treat it like an advertising cost.

Orcholski: We use eBay as a marketing tool. We make a little bit of money on it, but if it was our only avenue for sales, I would have gotten out of this business a long time ago.

EBay is a loss leader. You do make money on there, but the profit margins on eBay are slim compared to the amount of time I put into working it.

But the other things that it leads to make it worthwhile. You must have that continuous presence on eBay. EBay helped to put me in business.

Joyner: Are there any tips you have for being as profitable as possible on eBay, while minimizing those unavoidable costs of doing business?

Orcholski: You have to buy smart. That's the only way to ensure that you're profitable. You have to find reliable suppliers. You must get the best possible prices you can through your suppliers. Also, try to make a little bit of money on shipping, or at least enough to cover your costs.

That's probably the biggest complaint I hear from buyers. They don't like you to make money on shipping. In our case, we charge $4.50 for shipping the first coin and $1 for each additional coin. Typically, I cap shipping at $15 to $20, no matter how much you order. Our shipping is very reasonable compared to other sellers in our category. It should be more than what we're charging, but it would be too hard to pass on to the customer.

Postage can be anywhere from 39 cents to 80 cents. Plus, we've got our material and labor costs.

Power**Pointer**

Try to build in a slight profit in your shipping charges. At the very least, be sure to cover your costs.

Joyner: Even when you take into account labor, shipping supplies, and postage, you're still making some money on that $4.50 you're charging.

Orcholski: Maybe a buck, or a buck and a half.

Joyner: On what percentage of your eBay sales would that be the only profit you make?

Orcholski: Maybe 50 percent.

Joyner: So, in order to make a profit on eBay, you have to do more than simply control your listing costs and other fees. You contend that you have to have a great source of supply at good prices. In your case, do you get discounts for buying in large quantities?

Orcholski: I have a minimum order of usually $25,000. You have to buy in large quantities. You must buy smart in my business. The more you can buy, the higher the percentage you can save. If you can save 1 percent or 2 percent, that's going to drop right to your bottom line.

I deal in very slim profit margins. After all, some refer to eBay as "fleabay." They view it as a place to get good deals.

Joyner: Why do you think the mindset is so different on eBay? If I go to a company's web site and buy from them directly, I certainly expect that they'll make a profit. But on eBay, I expect a great deal above all else.

Orcholski: EBay was built on the reputation of being a flea market, and when you go to a flea market you expect to get things really cheap.

Joyner: Even die-hard coin collectors expect to pay less than market value when buying from you on eBay?

Orcholski: Yes.

Joyner: Talk to me about your web site and how that evolved. What made you decide that you needed a dedicated site for your business?

Orcholski: It's just that next logical extension to increase sales. You make more money on it. You can charge less than what you charge on eBay because you don't have to pay the eBay fees. I have to charge roughly 9 percent more to achieve the same level of profitability on eBay because of the eBay fees. I'm not obviously going to make less money, so I have to charge more.

We want to make a certain percentage regardless of where we sell our merchandise.

Power**Pointer**

In most cases, you will need to charge more to cover your costs on eBay, compared to sales made through your own dedicated web site. Compare your selling costs on both platforms and do the math to figure out just how much more you need to charge on eBay to earn the same amount. Then price your eBay auctions accordingly.

Joyner: Some sellers respond to fee increases by leaving eBay or changing how they list items for sale on the site, perhaps by shifting more listings to their eBay stores. But you don't do that. You simply raise your prices across the board.

Orcholski: If eBay wants to make more money, we want to make more money. If we can't, then we'll sell somewhere else. Where I sell it is immaterial, but I'm not going to sell an item at a loss on purpose.

So far, all of the changes and fee increases at eBay have worked to our advantage because we've lost competition.

Joyner: You seem to do an incredible amount of analysis of your business to determine exactly how profitable each marketplace is and what return you're getting on various expenses.

Orcholski: A lot of smaller sellers on eBay treat it as a hobby. PeSA members don't. You can't do that. You have to treat it as a business if you want to make it worth your while to do, unless you don't mind doing it for free or even losing money off it.

For those sellers who want to use eBay as a viable marketing alternative, you've got to watch your expenses. You've got to buy smart, and you've got to try to make money every single way that you can. Not a lot, but if you can make a dollar here and a dollar there, if you do enough business it all adds up.

PowerPointer

To make eBay a viable marketing alternative, you need to watch your expenses and make at least some money every way you possibly can.

Joyner: Given that some of your auctions close at 99 cents, and therefore at a loss, how are you able to sell $40,000 to $50,000 in merchandise every month on eBay?

Orcholski: Because there's also an element of human greed. You've heard the saying, "Greed is good"? Customers do get greedy and they get caught up in the bidding.

A lot of people who buy our things look at it as an investment. The things that we sell do have the very real potential to increase in value over time. That helps.

I also usually know how much we're going to make on each auction and what an item is going to bring in. I know what our costs are and what our shipping fees will be, and I usually know what we'll make before even listing an item.

Power**Pointer**

Calculate how much you expect to make for an item before you even list it.

Joyner: You've said before that auctions ending on Monday and Tuesday nights tend to close for less than those that close on other nights. Is it best to schedule your auctions to end on the weekends?

Orcholski: For me, the best ending times are Friday.

Joyner: Do you know why?

Orcholski: I don't. It used to be the worst day to end an auction. But now we have more auctions that end on Friday than on any other day of the week.

Joyner: You've apparently set the expectation among your customers that Friday is the day to check in on your auctions?

Orcholski: Yes. For probably three and a half years, we've had more auctions ending on Friday than on any other day. Saturday mornings are good. Sundays are okay. Mondays, Tuesdays, and Wednesdays are always the worst.

Joyner: When you have a lot of repeat buyers, you can train people to check your auctions on a regular basis.

Orcholski: For us, 65 percent of the people who bid on our auctions check our auctions once a day. About 80 percent of all those who look at our auctions on eBay look every three days, and a big chunk of them look every day.

Because we have so many repeat customers, we've learned to market to those customers and not to the eBay population in general.

Joyner: How do you market to your existing customers?

Orcholski: By putting our auctions up on a regular, predictable schedule.

Joyner: Knowing that people are coming back every one or three days to look at your auctions makes it especially important for you to list new merchandise for sale every day.

Orcholski: That's why we list something new every day.

PowerPointer

If you want a lot of repeat business, establish a reliable listing schedule, and continually post new items each day so customers will have a reason to keep coming back.

Joyner: So, even though Mondays aren't good days for you to have auctions end, you still need to put new merchandise up for bid on Mondays?

Orcholski: Yes. If you want eBay to be a successful sales channel, I have found that you must list every day, including holidays. The only night for sure that we don't have auctions end is Christmas Eve.

Joyner: What about Christmas night?

Orcholski: Yes. Christmas night is a good sales night. Remember, people can shop on eBay from the comfort of their own house.

We tend to end our auctions in the evening, usually around 8 or 8:30 central time.

People have been doing the Christmas thing all day, but maybe they'll go on their computer to do some shopping in the evening. At that time of the year, we have found that a lot of people are out looking to buy something for themselves.

Joyner: Back to the topic of fraud, which you touched on briefly earlier in our conversation, is the biggest issue for you that you must compete with fraudulent sellers? Or do you have to deal with fraudulent bidders, as well?

Orcholski: Both. Every year, we have two or three buyers through eBay who are fraudulent, most likely through a hijacked account. We get buyers who claim they never got the merchandise. That happens almost monthly. In most cases we can prove with delivery confirmation through the post office that they got the order.

The bigger concern is buyers who have been cheated by somebody else. These people leave eBay and never come back. Nevertheless, I've found that the majority of people who get cheated do come back to eBay. They're just more careful the next time.

Joyner: If you've gotten burned once, you don't want it to happen again. I can certainly understand that.

Orcholski: We have a lot of people who buy something small from us, like a silver coin that maybe costs $22 with shipping. Then we'll see their name again maybe a week or two later on a larger order.

Joyner: Sounds like they're testing the water. In the case where someone using a hijacked account defrauds you, are you able to recoup your financial losses?

Orcholski: Sometimes. If we ship to a PayPal confirmed address and we have proof of delivery, then PayPal will cover the loss.

Fraud is more of a worry for us on our web site because of stolen credit cards. On eBay, we've gotten better now at detecting fraudulent orders. We know what to look for.

It's a concern for our customers. When we've listed some more expensive items, our customers would get second-chance offers from someone claiming to be us. Of course they were frauds. A couple of customers unfortunately responded to these offers, and wound up losing money.

Joyner: But the offers appeared to come from you?

Orcholski: Yes. Now in our auctions, in big bold letters, we state that we do not extend second-chance offers on auctions. So, if they get one, it's a fraud. It's not from us.

Joyner: Before this started to happen, were you ever extending second-chance offers?

Orcholski: I would do them occasionally, but now I don't do them at all. That's another sales venue that we've lost because of fraud.

Joyner: I generally consider myself to be a pretty savvy eBay customer, but I'm not sure I would think twice about responding to a second-chance offer. I would assume it was a legitimate e-mail, not a phishing scam.

Orcholski: It tends to be on the higher-price items. If you do get such an offer, you've got to be careful. I would make sure that there's a phone number where you can contact the seller, especially if the item is of any sizable dollar amount.

Joyner: The phishing e-mails get more and more sophisticated all the time. These days, it's hard to tell the difference between them and legitimate communications from legitimate sellers.

Orcholski: You can't. We maybe get a couple dozen spam e-mails or spoofs every day.

PowerPointer

Watch out for fraud and possible phishing e-mail ploys, in which thieves send out e-mails trying to impersonate legitimate web sites in an effort to extract money from unsuspecting Internet users.

Joyner: It sounds like even with all the challenges you face on eBay, you're doing things right to keep your business going.

Orcholski: I hope so.

Let me offer this bit of advice: If you want to do this successfully, you have to answer all your e-mails, even the dumb ones. E-mails in our case are like getting phone calls, so you have to answer them all. If you're a bricks-and-mortar store, you're going to answer your phones when they ring. That's how I look at e-mail. I check it every 15 to 20 minutes. It's one of the last things I do before I go to bed, and it's one of the first things I do when I get up in the morning.

You have to give good customer service. You really do.

How true that is! When you start to think of e-mail as being equivalent to the phone ringing in your store, it only makes sense that you'll answer the call, because presumably a customer is on the other end of the line. By the same token, when customers e-mail a question or concern, make sure they get a personalized and complete response right away. I'm always amazed at the poor job many merchants do at responding to e-mail questions. How you reply, and how quickly, can often mean the difference between whether you make or lose a sale. So establish a strategy for replying to all e-mails. It will give you a significant competitive advantage.

$\sim$11$\sim$

Dan Yen

Movie Mars

Brothers-in-law Douglas Chen and Dan Yen were reluctant business partners. Although they married identical twin sisters, Chen and Yen don't have much in common when it comes to their outlook on business.

Chen, a busy physician, is definitely more of a realist in terms of money and business, even to the point of being downright pessimistic. Yen, by contrast, is an engineer by trade but an entrepreneur at heart. That means he's willing to take much bigger risks, especially if he thinks they will pay big rewards.

Despite these huge differences in philosophy and personality, Yen and Chen are partners in Movie Mars, a multimillion-dollar online venture that generates most of its revenues on eBay. Their company is perhaps the biggest media seller on the online auction web site, selling approximately $15 million worth of movies, music, and books on eBay every year at the rate of about 2,000 items every day. The company sells under the user IDs moviemarz and bookmarz.

Movie Mars, which is based in Charlotte, North Carolina, is an outgrowth of a fan web site started by the men's wives to honor their favorite movie, *Anne of Green Gables*. Visitors to that site soon began soliciting the twin sisters to start selling copies of the movie and other classic period films. To oblige their fans, they found a supplier and began selling copies of the movie through the web site.

It was actually Douglas Chen, the doctor, who suggested that there might be a moneymaking opportunity behind the sisters' hobby, especially if they started selling movies on eBay. Chen broached the subject with his brother-in-law and suggested they join together and start a little sideline business selling DVDs on eBay. But Yen wasn't interested in getting sucked into a small business. He was still in college at the time, studying for his master's degree, and didn't have time to waste on a small, upstart venture.

No matter. In what little free time he had from medicine, Dr. Chen kept the idea alive and for several years sold movies out of his one-car garage with moderate success.

When Yen finished his MBA, Dr. Chen finally convinced his brother-in-law to join him in business. Yen, being more of risk taker, accepted the job under one condition: Movie Mars needed to be a serious business. It also needed to become one of the biggest fish in the eBay pond.

With unparalleled speed, Movie Mars became exactly that. The company, which started with an inventory of just 2,000 titles, now has more than 1 million unique listings on eBay, a feat the business partners accomplished by embracing automation in every facet of their operation, including inventory management and warehouse operations. They keep costs in check with tight logistical controls and downright smart management oversight of every variable.

Yen, who is the company's chief executive officer (Dr. Chen kept his day job in medicine) shares the story of how Movie Mars became a Titanium PowerSeller almost overnight, and how their business continues to thrive in one of eBay's most competitive and lowest-margin categories.

Joyner: It's pretty amazing to think that this all started with a fan web site.

Yen: Yes, my wife put up an *Anne of Green Gables* movie fan site. Every day she'd get requests from people who thought that it was the official site that they could buy the movie from. After getting repeated requests from people interested in buying the movie, she actually found someone in Canada who would source the film. Then, her twin sister got involved and they built another web site, called Eras of Elegance (at www.erasofelegance.com), that featured period films. That's how we started selling period films.

Joyner: Does that web site still exist?

Yen: It does. It's really about different films from various periods in history, such as Jane Austen films and the like. They found a video supplier that would supply these films to them.

My sister-in-law's husband, who is a physician, came up with the idea of selling nonperiod films on the site. I didn't want to get involved because I was really busy in my schooling. So my brother-in-law started selling some other random films from his garage as a hobby and began to realize that he could make some money doing this.

He did that for a couple of years, and when I graduated from business school, he approached me with his business proposal again. He told me there were some large sellers on eBay and said, "There's no reason we can't become a large seller, too. Do you want to join me to try to build this business?"

Joyner: When your brother-in-law made that pitch to you, did you really think it was likely that you'd be able to build a multimillion-dollar business on eBay?

Yen: I think I've always been kind of an entrepreneur at heart and always an optimist, probably to the extreme. My brother-in-law is more of a realist. I call him a pessimist, but he calls himself a realist. The two of us make a great balance. At the time, I had just graduated with an MBA degree and said, "What's stopping us from becoming one of these large major sellers on eBay? We certainly can try, at least, and give it our best shot." And so that's when Movie Mars was born: June 1, 2004.

Joyner: What enabled Movie Mars to make the jump from a garage-based company to one of the largest media sellers on eBay?

Yen: Over the course of two years, when he was running the business out of his garage, my brother-in-law manually and painstakingly created auction ads for about 2,000 DVDs. He didn't have any automation, and there was no organization.

The moment we started the business, we began researching the tools that the large sellers on eBay were using. A lot of them were using a third-party software program called ChannelAdvisor to automate their operations. So we signed up with ChannelAdvisor as well. Doing so allowed us to basically load thousands of items for auction overnight. I think that's helped us to grow from selling a few items a day to selling many more. We credit our quick growth to the automation capabilities that the third-party software program gave us.

Power**Pointer**

In order to grow big, you'll need to automate your operations using a program such as ChannelAdvisor to load all of your auctions and manage your online inventory.

Joyner: How were you able to so quickly upload so many items for auction? Did you use a bar-code scanning system?

Yen: Yes. I actually spent some time programming and developing the whole scanning system. Bar codes obviously are the easiest way to track all your items.

Power**Pointer**

Using bar codes, which can be easily scanned, is an easy way to track all of your items.

Joyner: There's a lot of competition in the media categories on eBay. That means that profit margins can be pretty tight. As a result, merchants have to pay very close attention to their listing and selling costs. How do you list your movies for sale on eBay—in the auction format or in an eBay store?

Yen: The majority of items are in stores. That's just because it has been so inexpensive to list in stores. We have some items up for auction, but not a lot because the auction costs so much. However, with eBay stores' fees going up by more than 200 percent, up to 5 cents per item listing and sometimes up to 10 cents, we're going to be cutting listings quite a bit. I think that's pretty much what everyone is going to do in the category.

Joyner: In the DVD movies category on eBay, some big merchants— including at least one Titanium PowerSeller—have gone out of business. What are you doing to avoid that same fate?

Yen: I think what happened with the largest sellers like Laser Corner and Glacier Bay, which are no longer selling on the site, is that they were around for many years and essentially dominated the market. When the barriers to entry dropped, you had this influx of competition come in. Not only that, the competition came in with low overhead. In turn, profit margins dropped considerably. The large, entrenched sellers that were used to higher margins and overhead had difficulty adjusting to the influx of competition.

I kind of view it as being like what happened to United Airlines and American Airlines when JetBlue and Southwest Airlines entered the marketplace. These new entrants came in and had really low overhead. The larger, long-standing carriers had a hard time adjusting to that.

Power Pointer

Never become complacent. No matter how large or popular you get, new merchants with lower-cost ways of doing business may enter the market, undermining your business strategy. Think of how low-cost providers JetBlue and Southwest Airlines took passengers away from established carriers by coming up with cheaper and more efficient fare structures.

Joyner: You entered the business having lower profit margin expectations. Is that a fair statement?

Yen: That's definitely a fair statement.

The other thing is that, from the very beginning, we tried our best to keep our operating costs as low as possible, because we knew in order to survive in this business we just had to do that.

I was on a panel at eBay Live! and someone commented that it almost seems like you've got to clock your employees' every movement and tell them how to navigate your warehouse just to make sure that you have the most efficient process in place. And my answer was, "In essence, yes." This particular market evolved to the point where your costs just need to be managed extremely well. And if you don't do that, you're just not going to be competitive. Or you're not going to be able to stay in business.

Power Pointer

You must keep operating costs as low as possible, especially when selling commodity items.

Joyner: That's a very interesting point. It sounds like you're taking a cue from manufacturing plants and setting up very efficient processes in your warehouse, almost akin to an assembly line. Can you walk me through the process that employees in your warehouse go through when getting an order for shipment? How is this accomplished in the most efficient manner possible?

Yen: Although I'd rather not tell you exactly what happens for competitive reasons, I can say that Douglas and I spent a lot of time in the beginning of our operation sitting around and just watching what people do, where they're going, and for what reasons. And we asked ourselves, "How can we improve the logistics of the business, whether it be people movement or actual automated processes?" We considered a variety of factors—packing, standing, or shelving—and asked, "Is this the most efficient way to do it?"

I think that may have been a luxury to have that kind of time to sit, but we did that. We spent hours, sometimes in a heated debate, thinking about how things should be done.

I think that laid some good foundations in terms of establishing the ins and outs and logistics of the warehouse. I think that's very important to make sure you've got the most efficient model in place.

Joyner: I know this is probably a gross oversimplification, but it sounds a little bit like the things you might consider if you're designing a kitchen in your home. You want the refrigerator, stove, and sink in a triangle pattern because that's more efficient.

Yen: Definitely. It is a simplification, but in some ways it's not. You'd be surprised how simple your processes are that you're actually trying to analyze.

Think about the DVD business: You grab a DVD, put it in an envelope, slap a label on it, and it goes out the door. That whole process is fine and dandy for 10, or even 100, items a day. When you're dealing with 2,000 items a day, that simple one-two-three-step process is no longer so simple. It's really the scalability of it that kills you.

I think one of the competitive advantage in our business is being able to still do things simply even when you're moving 2,000 items a day. When we were in a one-car garage, it was faster to pack the same 100 items than when we first moved to a warehouse because of the fact that people had to walk around more.

Power**Pointer**

It's crucial to streamline your process for fulfilling orders, while making sure it is scalable as your company grows. One way to figure out what can be improved is to observe closely how you're doing things now and figure out where improvements can be made.

Joyner: You obviously had to figure out a way to minimize that. Often, eBay merchants selling in highly competitive categories like yours emphasize the importance of obtaining inventory at the absolutely lowest price, which I'm sure is a goal of yours, as well. But what do you think is more important: logistics or inventory cost?

Yen: I think the efficiencies gained operationally are probably of greater importance in a low-margin, high-volume business like ours.

Joyner: Do you get the sense that you and your competitors are pretty much getting the same wholesale prices from your suppliers?

Yen: I would think so, at least from my experience.

Joyner: How difficult will it be to maintain the same level of profitability given some of the changes on eBay, specifically the price hikes in eBay stores?

Yen: I've talked to some of my competitors on eBay—we often commiserate together. I think the general goal now is no longer growth and prosperity. It's survivability. It's viability. EBay's fee increases appear to be threatening the viability of this business model.

Joyner: Are you selling more off of eBay now through your own web site? Or is that a viable channel?

Yen: Sure. If you were to talk to everyone in my position or a similar position, they would all say, "I want to sell as much as possible off eBay"—especially the large media sellers.

But I think it's very difficult to drive customers to your web site. The bulk of our sales are still on eBay. From the eBay buyers' standpoint, they feel very comfortable on eBay. It's not easy to get buyers to buy directly from you, and even so, we would always sell on eBay as well.

EBay is a great form of marketing for your own dot-com. The company is out there spending millions of dollars on marketing to bring in customers. EBay is always going to be a huge value to companies like ours. I think that it's difficult to be a viable e-commerce company without eBay.

Power**Pointer**

While you want to steer as much business as possible to your own web site in order to cut down on selling fees, eBay will likely remain your largest sales channel. The site spends millions to attract buyers, and customers often feel more comfortable doing business there.

Joyner: How important is it to brand yourself on eBay, particularly in your category?

Yen: Because we're selling a real commodity item, I think branding has less value. It's more important to provide a good customer experience.

Joyner: I'd like to touch on that point more. Talk to me a little bit about the experience you try to create for your customers when they're buying from you on eBay.

Yen: We try our best, obviously, to get the product to the customer quickly. We offer a 30-day satisfaction guarantee and allow customers to return an item for a full refund, regardless of the item.

I think it's always a fine balance. You want to provide the best customer satisfaction, but you have to balance that with your costs. We're not selling Lexus cars, right? Sometimes you can go overboard with your customer service.

Power**Pointer**

Get products shipped quickly to customers and offer a 30-day satisfaction guarantee.

Joyner: If I bought something from you today on eBay, when would that item be shipped?

Yen: It would take a day or two to pack it, and then it should arrive in anywhere from three to five days in the United States.

Joyner: Because margins are so low on DVDs, CDs, and similar items, some sellers will ratchet up the shipping costs to ensure that they make a profit. What's your policy on shipping? How much do you charge?

Yen: We always try to charge people roughly what it takes to pack it and ship it. On eBay, some people will charge $8 just to ship a DVD. For us it's $4.50 and we arrived at that number because that's what the bulk of successful sellers on the site are charging and that's what customers are used to.

When we first started our business, we charged around $4. We benchmarked some large sellers to see what they were charging.

Power**Pointer**

To gauge how much to charge for shipping, check out what your major competitors are doing. Strive to deliver the same service for the same price or less.

Joyner: What about selling and shipping internationally? How big of a slice of your business is that?

Yen: I'd say international sales are about a fifth of our business. It's definitely significant.

Joyner: Did you make a conscious effort to market your products internationally or did it just kind of happen as you grew on eBay?

Yen: I think it just kind of happened. A lot of people internationally find our products, and you start to realize you're shipping to all these different places.

Joyner: Have you encountered any challenges in selling internationally? Are there places you won't ship or sell to?

Yen: We try to sell everywhere possible. But there are so many issues of fraud. To combat that, we look at orders that come in and if an order is over around $150, we'll screen it. If it's a large order, it will get flagged and we'll investigate the buyer to make sure they're legitimate before shipping anything to them.

To be honest, fraud is less of an issue for media sellers because the average cost of our items is $10 to $15. If people defraud us for that amount of money, often we just consider it to be the cost of doing business.

Joyner: I suppose it's not the same as if you're selling jewelry or cameras or some of those higher-ticket items, where a fraudulent order could cost you hundreds, if not thousands, of dollars.

Yen: Right.

Joyner: I've heard from other media sellers that they purposely don't carry new releases because they don't want to compete with stores like Wal-Mart and Best Buy. Are there certain titles that you don't carry because of competitive pressures?

Yen: I would agree with those sellers that new releases don't sell as well on eBay because you've got Target and Wal-Mart selling them as loss leaders. The titles I primarily sell are those you can't find in the stores.

But we don't limit ourselves. We will offer new releases and anything else that we can.

Joyner: Is that because you're really trying to be a one-stop shop for customers looking for DVD movies?

Yen: Definitely.

Joyner: When customers come to your eBay store, do you to try to get them to buy more than one DVD from you during that single online shopping trip?

Yen: ChannelAdvisor has an up-sell feature, and they'll rotate inventory through the checkout system and offer our customers a chance to buy complementary items as well. But that really hasn't been a major focus for us. One thing you realize as a small eBay company is there are a lot of great ideas; you just don't have the manpower and resources to implement them all. Or at least you just have to prioritize. Cross-selling is the big idea that we probably need to be focusing on, trying to grow our business from that standpoint. I always view Amazon as the benchmark for our business, and that's exactly what Amazon does.

Power**Pointer**

Always look for opportunities to cross-sell other complementary products to customers before they check out.

Joyner: How many different titles do you carry?

Yen: We have over a million unique titles, and four million listings on eBay, which I think is more than anyone on the site.

Joyner: You've been quoted as saying that you can run those million listings on autopilot. Is that really true?

Yen: I rarely have to deal with listings at all. It's all automated.

Joyner: Really, at this point, your only touch point is shipping. Is that correct?

Yen: You mean in terms of actually packing and shipping the item?

Joyner: Yes.

Yen: Yes. That's right. A lot of large media sellers drop ship. Contrary to what people think, we ship everything from our warehouse. Every single item that gets sold touches one of our packers' hands.

Joyner: Why did you opt not to go for the drop-ship model?

Yen: Mainly because we wanted control of the inventory. When you get people drop shipping for you from another supplier's warehouse and some other person that you don't really know is packing and shipping your items to your customers, you don't have a sense of control. You really have no quality management. We have extremely high standards and expectations of our business and of our employees, and we can't really put that kind of standard and expectation on people who drop ship.

We want to make sure an order is packaged and labeled right and that it's going out the door on time. If you try to start managing all these drop shippers, it becomes a nightmare.

Power**Pointer**

While drop shipping is always an option, it takes the quality control out of your hands.

Joyner: Can you give me an example maybe of how those high standards manifest themselves?

Yen: From the beginning, when we interview an employee, we tell him or her what kind of work environment it is and what kind of standards we expect.

I won't say exactly how we measure employees' performance, but we do have benchmarks in place and we usually put each employee on some type of probation—usually three months—so they can meet those benchmarks. It's understood that employees have a goal and they need to make this level of performance in order to fit in with the company.

Power**Pointer**

Set benchmarks for employees and put new hires on short-term probation to ensure they are able to meet those standards and fit in with the company.

Joyner: How many employees do you have now?

Yen: We currently have about 20.

Joyner: Are most of those warehouse employees?

Yen: Mostly, but we do have some senior software developers who work for us.

Joyner: Some readers might be surprised to hear that you have senior software developers on staff, especially because you're also using ChannelAdvisor auction management software. Can you talk to me a little about what you rely on your developers to do?

Yen: When we first started our company it was just Douglas, myself, and one other employee. We didn't have the luxury or the financial means to have professionals working for us.

But as your business grows, you realize that third-party software programs become a little more limited and you need to actually develop in-house programs and processes that allow for flexibility and scalability. That's what happened for us and why we have software developers on staff.

Joyner: So, they're programming solutions to make all your software applications work together? They're writing code that helps your auction management platform integrate with your shipping platform and so forth?

Yen: Right. I think it all goes back to scalability. There are plenty of great programs out there when you're dealing with lower volumes. But as you ratchet up in volume, you are forced to develop programs internally in order to keep up.

Power**Pointer**

While off-the-shelf software is great when you're starting out, as your business grows, you'll likely want to bring in outside experts to help you develop proprietary computer programs that more effectively scale your business.

Joyner: Not that you would ever invite competition, but do you think that the media category is one that at this point should be avoided? If someone wanted to go into business on eBay, would you recommend that they consider selling in the media category?

Yen: I would avoid it like a plague. In all honesty, I wake up in the morning and wonder, "Why am I selling DVDs? Why can't I be selling clothes?"—or something with higher profit margins, you know. When eBay calls and tells me they're raising fees, it's on those days that I really wonder what am I doing in this business.

Douglas and I have already vowed to each other that by the next eBay Live! we will not just be a DVD seller, because I think it's getting extremely difficult to maintain that going forward. It would just be nice if we were a little more diversified.

Joyner: As you look to diversify, are there certain items you're considering? Are there things that you've learned as a DVD and media seller that you can take to another category? For example, one eBay merchant who sells antiques and unique items told me she really envies companies like Movie Mars because you have fairly fixed shipping costs and can send items out in the same sized box. Are you keeping those things in mind as you look for that next opportunity?

Yen: Yes. But I think the biggest thing you need to consider when sourcing products is that customers want to know exactly what they're going to get when they buy online. I think that's why commodities like DVDs, CDs, and books sell so well. Finding something else that generates that much consumer confidence is the first thing in our minds in terms of finding another product. We certainly haven't come up with anything yet.

Power**Pointer**

Consumers like to know exactly what they're buying—and what they'll get—when buying online. It's one reason commodity items like books and DVDs sell so well. But these are also the most crowded and competitive categories.

Joyner: From the sourcing side, do you think it will be difficult to find suppliers to sell to you when you do move to diversify your inventory? And contrast that to what you encountered when you were first starting out in business.

Yen: It should definitely be easier now. I would think that our current business on eBay lends a level of credibility in terms of being a serious company that can move a large volume of items.

Credibility is an all-important word. You need credibility to build up credit with your suppliers, as well as to earn the trust of potential buyers. It's something that doesn't come overnight, so be ready to work hard and go the extra mile in order to build a solid reputation for your business.

Incidentally, the concept of moving into other product lines is something you should keep in mind when naming your business. "Movie Mars," for instance, would likely be limited to expanding into other areas related to movies, such as movie memorabilia, movie soundtracks, and so forth. A more generic name like "Amazon" could apply to just about anything. So, if you think there's a chance you may want to broaden your product offerings over time, go with something broad enough at the start so you won't have to rebuild your brand—and credibility—all over again as you expand into new areas.

12

Jacob North

Sophias Style Boutique

Jacob and Belinda North's eBay success story began like many others—with two working parents who wanted to be able to spend more time with their newborn.

The Norths had just welcomed their first child, daughter Sophia. Belinda quit her job to stay at home with Sophia. Jacob, who owned an Outback Steakhouse franchise, became the family's sole breadwinner.

As any new parent knows, raising a new baby is expensive. Plus, first-time parents can get carried away buying adorable clothing and other items for their newborns. The Norths were no different. From the moment she was born, Sophia had a closetful of clothes. As a growing baby will do, she outgrew many of these cute outfits quickly, long before they ever showed any wear.

As a hobby and to earn a little extra spending money, Belinda began selling Sophia's hand-me-downs on eBay under the user ID sophias*style. The couple's intent was never to make lots of money, but just to clear out Sophia's closets once she outgrew her clothes.

It wasn't long before the Norths got caught up in the intoxicating allure of eBay. Sophia's old clothes were selling quite well on the auction site for higher prices than the Norths ever imagined. Within six months, Jacob and Belinda realized that this hobby had the potential to be something more—much more.

And so it has become in just four short years.

The Norths have carved out a profitable niche as a boutique retailer of upscale clothing for little girls, both on sites like eBay and Amazon.com and through their own web site at www.sophiasstyle.com.

Within the past year, Jacob North left the restaurant business to devote himself to the online venture full-time, and the couple recruited two friends to join them as business partners in Sophias Style Boutique.

Their company now sells thousands of items every week, and this Platinum eBay PowerSeller is on a trajectory to grow even larger. A recent decision to begin using ChannelAdvisor software for auction and inventory management resulted in a 500 percent spike in sales in just a few months, and cleared the way for Sophias Style Boutique to sell in other online channels beyond eBay. Those channels now account for about 40 percent of the company's overall total. Every month, sales continue to increase.

For now, Sophias Style Boutique is still a small company. Every expense is carefully debated, weighed, and measured before being undertaken. That's one reason the business remains based out of the Norths' home in Bellevue, Nebraska. Moving to a larger warehouse doesn't yet make financial sense.

But Jacob North has big dreams for his company. "I hope one day we're Macy's and I get to work out of a skyscraper," he says.

In this chapter, Jacob North tells the story behind the steady yet fast growth of Sophias Style Boutique, a company that evolved from a couple's desire to dress their daughter in the very best. Their story should be quite inspirational for those of you just getting started, as they show how one can experience fast success if you choose the right niche product.

North also shares his views on how customer service can make or break an eBay business. Though it operates exclusively online, Sophias

Style Boutique models itself after upscale boutiques and the country's best department stores.

Joyner: How and why did you make the leap from hobby to business?

North: It really wasn't part of the initial plan. This was Belinda's hobby. She did it at night, and it was fun to watch what bidders would pay for certain items. Then we realized maybe we should really try to make some money off of this. We started doing a little research and found several distributors and a few manufacturers that would sell to us.

On eBay there was a lot of used children's clothing and cheaper brands available. We decided to do something different. We wanted to sell only new, higher-quality items that are packaged really nicely. We also saw a lot of gouging on shipping. The price would be cheap, but then you'd read the fine print and it's $15 to ship it to you.

We decided to focus on shipping, both by charging a fair price and by concentrating on exemplary packaging. We wrap every order in pink tissue paper and our customers get little extras like stickers and potpourri sachets in their packages.

Power**Pointer**

As an added value, pack little extras inside your packages as freebies for customers.

Joyner: Where did you get the idea for those little touches like the pink paper and the potpourri?

North: Department stores. In Omaha, Nebraska, one of the nicer places to go shopping is Bon Marché (now Macy's). Whenever you buy something, they wrap it up in front of you and put it in a nice box. Our goal on eBay was always to be on the high end to give you the department store or boutique store feeling, without charging a ton of money.

During our first six months of being in a serious business, our goal was never to make a lot of money. Our goal was to build up our feedback and reputation with suppliers so we could buy products at cheaper prices.

Joyner: Your business has certainly experienced tremendous growth over the last few years. To what do you attribute your success?

North: EBay is an incredibly tough marketplace to do business on, but what we think makes us successful is really simple. If somebody e-mails you, you answer them fast, hopefully within about a half hour. If somebody wants to make a return, you don't beat them up for it, even if they tell you some silly story about how the tags have come off and the outfit somehow just exploded on the little girl and they don't know how the clothing fell apart, but it did. You give them their money back once and let them know the return policy for next time.

I took that lesson from Outback: The customer really is always right, even on eBay.

It has always been our philosophy to send a nice product in a lovely package and send it fast. We ship everything within, at the latest, 24 hours of an order.

Fast shipping, nice shipping, good product, fair price—I'm sure you hear that over and over. It's really that simple. It's like my first boss at Outback said: "You don't have to be smart to run a restaurant. All you have to do is get the food out on time with a smile and everything will be fine."

Power**Pointer**

Even on eBay, the customer is always right.

Joyner: Many people have a hard time with that concept.

North: Well, those simple ingredients are absolutely required to run a successful business. I don't care if you're selling toilet paper or door-knobs. They really work.

Joyner: You also mentioned that it's your goal to answer all customer e-mails within 30 minutes of receiving them. Why is that so important?

North: At Outback, we used to ask our servers to greet the table within 30 seconds of the diners being seated and then within 30 seconds of food arriving at the table to see if anything was wrong. The same principle applies online. Answering e-mail just has to be a priority.

During business hours, which are 9 A.M. to 5 P.M. central time, we try to answer e-mails very quickly because if you don't either you're losing a sale or, if someone has a problem, you can usually turn the negative into a positive by getting back to them quickly.

Power**Pointer**

All e-mails should be answered quickly. Otherwise, you risk losing the sale or turning a negative situation into something even worse.

Joyner: How many customer e-mails would you estimate you get per day?

North: The least we ever get is 50, and the most, probably, is around 200.

Joyner: And how many people are answering those? The four business partners?

North: The four of us rotate through and answer them.

Joyner: Do you ever use form or automated messages to respond to customers' e-mail questions?

North: We do get asked a lot of the same questions over and over again. You can use automated systems to respond to e-mail messages, but we always try to tailor our response to the person. You can write a really good automated response, but it still looks automated.

Joyner: Why did you decide to start all your eBay auctions at a penny opening bid?

North: Our thought was that people always tend to look for the best deal. There are only four ways to sort search results on eBay—ending soonest, newly listed, highest-priced, and lowest-priced.

Starting each auction at a penny gives us a little more exposure. Maybe that penny opening bid will get us an extra five or six bidders. Obviously, some are not serious bidders, but it does generate a little more energy around the item.

Everybody wants to find that bargain for a dollar or a penny. That's how eBay is. Everybody wants to get a deal on eBay, and sometimes they do, but sometimes they don't.

Joyner: What can you do to minimize the number of items that you sell for a penny? Obviously you want the product to get bid up to a higher price, but sometimes it doesn't, despite your best marketing efforts.

North: The best thing you can do is pick the right product. It doesn't matter if you're Sophias Style or Macy's, when you go and pick out the new clothing lines, you're trying to pick good lines. That means not selecting what everybody else has; it means trying to make yourself different from everybody else out there and trying to be on the cutting edge of fashion, even in little girls' fashion. If you pick the wrong item or a brand that a lot of other sellers carry on eBay, you're going to have a tough go of selling it.

Joyner: Are you selling items exclusively for girls or have you added little boys' clothing into the mix now?

North: We tried little boys' clothing, and it didn't work so well for us. It may be that parents aren't willing to spend as much money on a little boy for clothing. Perhaps they think that boys will destroy them, so why bother? And little boys' clothing is so similar, it's hard to find anything different than what you could buy from Old Navy and Gap. It didn't work well for us, so we are focusing strictly on little girls' clothing now.

Joyner: Does your own little girl help with your market research? How involved is Sophia in choosing products? How much do you take into account her opinions when you're buying products?

North: She's four now, but she tends to think of everything as being cute, and she doesn't like anything with pants. Basically you get the same opinion from her all of the time!

Joyner: I know that children very early on develop a sense of fashion and can be quite vocal about what they like and don't like.

North: Yeah, she's got a one-track mind as far as what she likes and doesn't like is concerned. We'll ask her about certain products and if she just walks away from something after seeing it, that is something to keep in mind.

Power**Pointer**

Get feedback on your merchandise from your target market to make sure what you plan to sell is of interest to them.

Joyner: You've referenced your experience at Outback Steakhouse quite a bit. How much has that helped as you started your own business?

North: I think Outback's a fantastic company. They focus on the right things. If you worry about Jake or Annie when they sit down at the dinner table, your business will be okay.

I don't think it matters whether you're selling steaks, computers, or little girls' clothing, the minute you forget about the customer or don't treat them like they're someone special, they will go somewhere else.

Everybody is looking for a restaurant where they take care of you, or they're looking for a store where they take care of you.

No matter what you're selling, you must have good customer service.

Power**Pointer**

Regardless of what you're selling, the minute you forget about the customer or don't treat them as if they are special, they will go elsewhere.

Joyner: Do you think people are necessarily getting that on eBay, in general?

North: No. All you have to do is read the policies that companies put out there. They can be really antagonistic toward customers. Sometimes the policies sellers put out there are almost threatening: "If you bid on this item and don't pay, I'll leave you a negative feedback."

Why is eBay different from a department store? What do you lose if a customer changes her mind and doesn't pay? Who cares? You get your fees back and then you can put the item back up for sale.

Joyner: So, you wouldn't necessarily leave negative feedback for a non-paying bidder?

North: I think we've left 25,000 feedbacks and I think out of those two were negative, only because they were larger orders and winning bidders didn't respond to our e-mails.

Power**Pointer**

Don't write up policies for your site that are clearly anticustomer, such as "If you bid on this item and don't pay, I'll leave negative feedback for you."

Joyner: I'm looking at one of your items that you have for sale on eBay, and notice that you use a template for every auction that includes such information as the manufacturer's suggested retail price, the clothing's measurements, fabric content, and washing instructions. Why include all those details?

North: Our template has evolved over time. Customers will tell you what they want. If you get 5,000 e-mails from customers wanting to know the length of a dress or the retail value, you should pay attention.

Power**Pointer**

Pay attention to what your customers are saying and asking. If relevant, address those concerns in your auction listings.

Joyner: Anyone who's ever bought clothing can tell you that sizes vary by manufacturer, which makes shopping for them online difficult. Is that also true with children's clothing?

North: Yes. You're going to have some brands running differently than others.

Joyner: Does that cause you problems or a lot of returns?

North: When we didn't put the actual clothing measurements in the description, it caused a lot of returns.

Joyner: Do you take your own auction photographs?

North: We do.

Joyner: How many photos would you normally include in an ad?

North: It depends on what it is. If it's a hair bow, it gets one image. If it's an expensive dress that retails for $70, we'll put six images on there, showing the dress from every angle so that even though the customers can't touch it, they get as close as they can to touching it.

Joyner: I notice that you incorporate cross-selling techniques into your auction listings. When I'm looking at one of your auctions, I'm also given the option of completing the look. I can buy a coordinating hair clip or have the item monogrammed for $8. How does offering these kinds of add-ons affect your revenues?

North: In any business, everybody tries to cross-sell. The pizza guy asks if you want to buy a two-liter pop.

It's the same thing that happens when you go to a clothing store and at the checkout register you see little stuff for sale. That's how we got the idea.

All of our ideas come from traditional retail. I guess we're not incredibly creative. Why does the Internet have to be so different? Why can't there be up-selling? They do it at restaurants and everywhere else; why can't we do it?

Joyner: Is it hard to do up-selling or cross-selling with eBay? Or does the auction site's technology make it pretty easy to link complementary items to an auction?

North: No, it's not easy. We created the template that allows us to cross-sell within our auctions.

Joyner: But it certainly sounds like that programming investment pays off for you every day.

North: Yeah, I think so.

Joyner: Even so, up-selling as you're doing it isn't a completely automated process, right? Someone has to look at your inventory and determine which items are complementary to one another?

North: Yes. The computer can't match up the right shade of pink on an outfit to the right shade of pink on a hair clip. So, there are some man-hours that go into that.

PowerPointer

Automate a process for up-selling like and complementary items to your customers.

Joyner: You took a big risk by leaving a good job to become an online entrepreneur. Had you not left Outback and devoted yourself full-time to the eBay business, do you think you would be as successful as you are right now?

North: I don't think anybody can do anything successfully without fully devoting themselves to it and taking a risk. Either it's a sideline job, and you have to be happy with that, or it's your full-time business.

Joyner: How scary is it knowing that your family's financial well-being is riding on your eBay venture?

North: I would by no means say that we're secure or anything such as that. I know there are some Titanium PowerSellers that are just a couple of maneuvers away from going out of business. And I keep that in mind. I know we're a couple of bad decisions away from going out of business. But Belinda has a saying: "We're going to grow this company slowly and cautiously, as fast as we can." That's kind of what we try to do.

Power**Pointer**

Grow your company slowly and cautiously—as fast as you can.

Joyner: That's a good mindset. So far it seems to be working for you. You've experienced tremendous growth and some incredible successes in a very short time. Not many eBay merchants have reached Platinum PowerSeller status as fast as you have.

North: When you're in business for yourself, you just keep doing better. I don't really worry about when or if we'll become a Titanium PowerSeller, for instance. Growth is a good problem to have, and if it happens to us and we do become Macy's and huge—fantastic. But I think that's putting the cart a little in front of the horse.

I really admire North's down-to-earth approach. He's focused on creating the best experience possible for customers, knowing that this should lead to continued growth of his business. He's following the example set by many venerable bricks-and-mortar retailers. I, for one, definitely believe that online retailers should strive to offer outstanding customer service.

Focusing exclusively on getting big fast has led to the demise of many companies, including most of the early dot-coms that flamed out in the late 1990s. That is something to definitely keep in mind as you start to build your own eBay empire.

FIFTY SECRETS OF THE
eBAY BILLIONAIRES' CLUB

1. Step one in starting a successful company—even one based exclusively online—is to write a comprehensive and well-thought-out business plan.

2. Instead of drawing income from your business, especially at the start, reinvest the profits into more inventory so your company can grow even bigger.

3. Getting bonded through a company such as BuySafe is one way to increase confidence among potential buyers.

4. The key to scaling your business and selling in volume is having an effective automated auction management program.

5. Consider listing similar items for sale at the same time. That way, the auctions end in sync and you can concentrate on stuffing packages of the same size and specifications, making your shipping operation more efficient.

6. A good strategy for moving merchandise is to start auctions at 99 cents. This low starting price point will also save you money in listing costs and it will attract more bidders, effectively driving up the prices on your auctions.

7. One way to get started selling on eBay is by becoming a trading assistant or selling on consignment for others. The primary advantage is that you won't have to make a huge initial investment of money in order to obtain inventory.

8. Read the "Announcements" message board in eBay's Community section each day to get the latest on what's happening throughout the site.

9. It's better to start the bidding at a higher price than to use reserves. Reserves can discourage people from placing a bid in the first place.

10. Be open to accepting all forms of payment, including money orders, PayPal, credit cards, cashier's checks, and services such as Google Checkout. For personal checks, wait for the funds to clear before shipping the item.

11. Feedback is reciprocal. Leave feedback as soon as you receive payment for an item. If a customer leaves negative feedback about your company, respond appropriately. Be courteous and understanding, not negative and sarcastic.

12. The eBay Giving Works program is a great way for small online businesses to establish a connection and donate a percentage of profits to their favorite charities. Participating in the program can also bring more traffic to your auctions. Unless you're looking to donate all of your proceeds to charity, 10 percent of the total sale price is a good amount to earmark for a good cause.

13. Consider setting up shop in multiple online venues, not just on eBay, to reach the broadest number of customers.

14. Motivate customers to buy multiple items from you at the same time by offering free or combined shipping charges.

15. When you're selling merchandise, the faster you turn it over, the greater your profits.

16. Use eBay's Marketplace Research area or data analysis tools from companies like Terapeak and HammerTap to figure out which items are most likely to sell best.

17. Avoid relisting items. If an item doesn't sell the first time you list it for sale on eBay, discount the price significantly so you quickly get rid of the item and bring in better-selling, more profitable merchandise.

18. There's no need to always stick with just one pricing strategy. You can change your approach, depending on what you think will work best for a particular item.

19. Among the variables to consider when deciding whether to stock an item for sale: How easily can it be shipped? After all, shipping charges can sometimes cost more than the merchandise itself, instantly turning off any potential buyers.

20. When selling heavy or bulky merchandise, consider offering flat-rate shipping to ease the minds of buyers concerned about how much it will cost to have the item delivered.

21. Include as many details as possible about your items in the written description, so you use all the possible keywords a potential buyer might search for. You may also want to include some common misspellings at the bottom of the page, just in case some bad spellers are looking for what you have to offer.

22. When selling commodity items, such as DVDs and some consumer electronics, it's generally wise to stock up on as many like products as possible, given the amount of work it takes to create an auction listing for each one.

23. When selling used merchandise, such as computers, establish minimum specifications that the products must meet in order to be in salable condition, and clearly communicate these standards to buyers so they know exactly what they're bidding on.

24. Always follow up with customers by e-mail and other means. Also, put marketing materials about your company, including other products you sell, in with each shipment.

25. In most cases, it's tough to generate repeat business on eBay because so many shoppers on the site are primarily concerned about price. Therefore, if you have your own web site, try to steer future business to this channel instead.

26. Brand-name merchandise that buyers are familiar with almost always sells better—and for more money—than off-brand merchandise.

27. Check out eBay's "plogs" for tips from other sellers on various issues, such as how to spot fake merchandise.

28. Answer e-mail queries from potential buyers promptly—and always within 24 hours. Treat responding to e-mail the same as answering the telephone in a bricks-and-mortar business.

29. Avoid having auctions end at times when you will not be in front of the computer. You want buyers to be able to e-mail last-minute questions to you and get an answer right up to the close of the auction.

30. It's critical that your auction listing contains both compelling content and photographs. Still, write the content description as if there were no photographs, and vice versa.

31. Avoid using flowery and wordy descriptions. Be straight and to the point when describing an item.

32. When offering merchandise with high initial listing fees, extend second-chance offers to runner-up bidders. This will save you from having to pay the high listing fee all over again.

33. One of the most effective ways to instill confidence in buyers is to offer a full refund if they are unsatisfied for any reason.

34. If you have any flexibility with high-priced items, consider using eBay's "Make Offer" or "Best Offer" features, which give buyers some wiggle room for haggling.

35. Network with other successful eBay sellers so you can share and benefit from the experiences of more veteran online merchants. Consider becoming a member of the Professional eBay Sellers Alliance and join the eBay community forum for sellers in your particular niche. You'll be able to get advice and share best practices with those who have more experience on eBay, as well as entrepreneurs who are selling in the same category.

36. You must keep operating costs—and this includes fixed over-head and eBay fees—as low as possible, especially when selling commodity items.

37. Always look for opportunities to cross-sell other complementary products to customers before they check out.

38. If you have a company location outside of your home and are looking to convince a manufacturer to do business with you, invite a representative over to meet with you on-site so the rep can see you are a serious entrepreneur capable of selling a lot of merchandise.

39. When searching for an auction management software provider, an important variable to consider is whether the company is reliable. Otherwise, a failure on its part can shut down your entire operation.

40. If you have a large supply of the same item, one strategy is to auction some off, while putting the rest for sale through your eBay store at a Buy It Now price. The auctions will drive traffic to your eBay store.

41. You can build an international presence cost effectively by out-sourcing the warehousing and shipment of your merchandise to a company based in the local country. Just be sure to do your homework first, because it's not easy finding legitimate foreign businesses with which to partner.

42. When shipping to international addresses, consider working with a mail consolidator, which already has negotiated rate contracts with postal services in foreign countries.

43. Keep track of questions frequently asked by your customers, and include the answers in your auction listings.

44. If you're selling for other people, set your commission fees high enough to recover all your costs, including eBay listing fees, eBay final-value fees, PayPal fees, your time, and your expertise.

45. Pay the extra 35-cent fee to include a gallery photo with your auction listing. These thumbnail-sized pictures show up on eBay's category listings and on search results pages, and they'll help your auctions stand out from the competition.

46. When selling an expensive item that is in high demand, consider running it as a featured auction. You'll pay an extra $19.95, but doing so guarantees your auction top-of-the-marquee billing on category listing pages and search pages on eBay. Before paying the extra fee to feature an auction, research the closing prices for similar items to make sure you'll be able to recoup the extra money you're spending on the listing.

47. Take advantage of eBay specials and offers. Several times a year, the web site lowers its listing fees to a penny. Other times, eBay may allow sellers to include gallery images or bold text in their auction titles for free.

48. If you make a mistake, respond promptly and correct the problem. If an item didn't ship out when it was supposed to, offer your customer free shipping. If an item was defective or if the wrong item was shipped, offer the customer a refund or a replacement, if available. Consider throwing in a few extra dollars for the customer's trouble.

49. Schedule your auctions to end when traffic is highest on eBay. Sunday evening is often a high-traffic time. Keep in mind that people on both coasts will be surfing on the site, so make sure your auctions end at times that are convenient in both the eastern and Pacific time zones.

50. Don't drive yourself crazy worrying about making a profit on every single item you sell on eBay. Instead, aim to be profitable in the aggregate and accept that you may have to sell some things at a loss to attract bidders' interest and make room for more inventory.

HOW I PUT TEN CRUCIAL STRATEGIES FROM *THE eBAY BILLIONAIRES' CLUB* TO WORK IN MY OWN BUSINESS (AND TRUST ME, THEY REALLY WORK!)

While I've written three books about how to prosper on eBay, my pursuits as a merchant on the site have always been more of a sideline than anything else. After all, I'm a writer first and foremost. But the tremendous success of those featured in my books has always amazed and inspired me. Writing *The eBay Billionaires' Club*, in particular, moved me to dip my feet deeper into the eBay waters than ever before. And guess what? By using the proven strategies and sales techniques of successful eBay merchants, I've been able to build an increasingly successful eBay business. In fact, I'm well on my way to becoming a PowerSeller.

First, a bit of background on how I got to this point. I've been a member of eBay for a decade, having first been introduced to the site in 1997 by a photographer friend named Mike. The two of us worked together at a newspaper in Augusta, Georgia. One day, while driving back from an assignment, we started talking about yard sales, a passion we both shared. Whereas I frequented garage sales and flea markets for the bargains, Mike scouted them for inventory that he could resell on eBay. Mike told me he earned an extra $500 a month selling things on eBay. That seemed like a fortune to me as a cash-strapped young reporter! So, as soon as I got home that night, I logged onto the Internet (that was back in the days of dial-up connections) and surfed over to eBay.

To say I was immediately hooked is an understatement.

I was amazed by this dynamic marketplace where you could seemingly find anything you wanted. (That has become even more true since then, as eBay's popularity and scope have grown enormously.) When I first discovered eBay, I had just begun a collection of vintage McCoy pottery, which was initially manufactured in the 1930s. My collection was very small and each piece was hard-won—usually a serendipitous discovery made in a dusty antique store or at an estate sale. EBay, however, offered a vast selection of McCoy flowerpots, vases, and bowls in shades of pastel pink, green, and yellow. Almost immediately, I began bidding on auctions, thrilled at how easy it was to build my collection through eBay. (It was surprisingly easy to do business with honest strangers from around the world.)

Though I wanted to follow in Mike's footsteps and earn money by selling on eBay, I didn't try this right away. My slow dial-up connection speed was one factor. Another was the fact that selling on eBay was hard back then (or at least more difficult than it is now). That was, after all, before the proliferation of digital cameras. If you wanted to post a photo online, you had to either scan the images yourself or have the developer save them to a CD. All that seemed too time-consuming.)

Nevertheless, I remained a devoted fan of eBay and over the years purchased hundreds of items on the site—pottery, books, CDs, DVDs, shoes, handbags, and even wedding favors. Once I had a digital camera and high-speed Internet service, I began selling a few odds and ends as well. Like many members of The eBay Billionaires' Club, I started out with used items and my own unwanted collectibles, more as a means of clearing out the closet than making money. But something happens when the money starts rolling in, even in small amounts. You begin thinking of eBay as more than just a hobby!

In the midst of writing my first book about the strategies of eBay's top merchants, *The eBay Millionaire*, I began ratcheting up my own eBay business. I started frequenting yard sales and going-out-of-business sales in order to buy inventory to resell on the global auction site. My husband and I even converted an oversized storage closet in our house into "the eBay room," to hold merchandise and packing supplies. After clocking out from our day jobs, we'd spend hours every night processing orders. Lunch breaks, meanwhile, were devoted to standing in line at the post office waiting to mail out the previous night's orders.

In my first attempt at running an eBay business, I employed many of the strategies advocated by eBay's top sellers. I used auction management software and templates to save time on every listing. I purchased a new digital camera and a scanner so I could post images of every item I was selling. I began most of my auctions at 99 cents, hoping to benefit from the bidding momentum that occurs when you open with a low starting price.

Admittedly, we did make a little bit of money from our eBay venture. But both my husband and I found our eBay business, in its first incarnation, too difficult to sustain while holding down our full-time jobs and maintaining a household. So, after we sold off most of our initial inventory, we decided to take a break.

After regrouping and reanalyzing the techniques of eBay's cream of the crop, The Style Channel by Amy was born. Upon reflection, I realized that although I followed some of the strategies I learned from the site's top merchants, we made a lot of mistakes during our first venture. Even though I literally wrote the book on eBay (three of them, actually), I didn't fully embrace *all* of the strategies for success that the PowerSellers advocate. Once I did, everything changed for the better. To save you time on this learning curve, here are the 10 strategies that have really helped to propel my eBay business.

Strategy One: Choose the Best Business Model

I'm now wiser and much savvier in my approach to eBay entrepreneurism. I'm building a successful online business with the help of mentors like David Yaskulka of Blueberry Boutique, Dan Glasure of Dan's Train Depot, Connie Gray of Estate Treasure by Byrum, Nir Hollander of Gem Stone King, Jacob North of Sophias Style Boutique, and the other sellers you've read about in these pages, along with those featured in my two previous books about online entrepreneurism (*The eBay Millionaire* and *The Online Millionaire*).

Let me first tell you a little bit about my new business, which varies greatly from my initial attempt on eBay. Before, I purchased merchandise to resell on eBay, but this time I've embraced a trading assistant/consignment business model, which has been employed so successfully by Adam Hersh Auctions, AACS Autographs, Express-Drop, and occasionally Exel-i. A friend of mine, a former manufacturer's sales rep, contracted with me to sell her product samples on eBay. I handle all the hard work of photographing and listing the items for sale, as well as shipping them out, and we share in the profits once all expenses have been paid. Although there are other lucrative eBay business models, this one works particularly well for me because I don't have to tie up money in inventory that might not sell. Because I am insulated from financial risk, I feel free to be more aggressive in pricing and in promotions that will attract customers.

My friend, who owns the inventory, is satisfied with the arrangement as well. She has a notoriously short attention span—a trait she readily admits—and is therefore happy to leave the time-consuming task of selling on eBay to me. What's more, she's not an experienced eBay user, so she doesn't understand the nuances of selling on the site. Lastly, she's excited to be able to clear these products out of her home and storage facility and to recoup some money from them.

Before we came up with the idea of selling on eBay, she planned to spend several weekends hawking them at a flea market at greatly reduced prices. We're earning significantly more money on eBay. In fact, my friend's goal is to use her portion of the profits to make improvements to her house. I haven't yet decided how to spend my newfound eBay wealth, which is growing incrementally every day.

Strategy Two: Treat It Like a Business

Too often, people approach selling on eBay as a hobby. If you want to make real money doing this, you must operate like a real business.

That means doing your due diligence before you even begin selling. Learn as much as you can about your merchandise and the demand for it before you post it for sale. Before I agreed to consign my friend's merchandise, I used eBay's Marketplace Research to find out what the demand was like for these items and to assess the competitive landscape.

Like Jim Orcholski of J&T Coins, I track every financial metric to determine how my business is doing and how specific products are performing. I do this using eBay's Selling Manager tools, along with the various spreadsheets I have developed. This does require an investment of time and small monthly financial outlay for Selling Manager, but I've found the benefits far outweigh the cost.

Strategy Three: Be Responsive

Operating like a real business also means paying attention to your customers and treating them well. I try to respond promptly—within a few hours—to all bidder or buyer questions. My BlackBerry helps me reply to e-mails even when I'm away from my computer. I've been known to thumb-type a reply in the waiting room of the doctor's office or in the checkout line at the grocery store. But even if you don't have portable e-mail access, you should still check your account several times a day to stay on top of customer concerns. As Jim Orcholski so accurately points out, not answering your eBay e-mail is like not answering the phone at a bricks-and-mortar business—unthinkable!

This prompt attention to customer care also applies to shipping. My rule is this: If I receive payment by 5 P.M., the item goes out with the next day's mail. On busy days, this can be a challenging standard to maintain, but it's very important for customer satisfaction. In my case, superfast shipping has helped me to capture some repeat customers. Many eBay buyers will note shipping speed, either positive or negative, in their feedback.

Strategy Four: Sell What You Know

Before, I sold just about everything on eBay—pottery, action figures, vintage magazines, kids' Halloween costumes, DVDs—as long as I had a hunch it might find an audience of bidders. Some of those items sold for a nice profit, but others languished in our upstairs eBay room. (Note to self: It's time to clean out that room!)

This time, I'm sticking to just a few product categories in areas in which I already have some expertise. Because I'm a consumer of cosmetics, beauty products, jewelry, and handbags, for example, I am much more adept at selling them. I know what these products are worth, what customers want, and what they are willing to pay for them, both on eBay and in more traditional marketplaces. I'm able to anticipate bidders' questions and write descriptions addressing those issues and, in turn, luring bidders in.

As Adam Hersh says, it is important for a trading assistant to bring not just eBay marketing expertise, but product expertise as well.

Strategy Five: Size Matters

My original "kitchen sink" approach to selling caused us some real shipping headaches. Some nights, we spent hours wrapping fragile collectibles in bubble wrap. Scrounging up appropriately sized boxes was also a challenge. I remember one occasion when we searched the local Wal-Mart Dumpsters for a box big enough to fit a large framed print! We ended up losing money on that sale because we didn't charge the winning bidder enough to ship the oversized object. Lesson learned the hard way.

No more. This time around, all of our merchandise is similarly sized, meaning it fits neatly into the same standard boxes, which can be purchased cheaply online. Our postage expenses are predictable as well, with almost everything costing $4.05 to ship via Priority Mail.

Selling similarly sized merchandise also streamlines the handling process. We now use an assembly-line process: Cosmetics are placed in zippered bags, wrapped in bubble wrap, and packed in boxes with foam peanuts or air bubbles. Such a routine translates into a real time savings. It's easy to process multiple orders quite quickly.

I owe this technique to Anthony Roberts, who has employed it successfully at AACS Autographs, and to Bruce Hershenson of eMovie

Posters.com, who was profiled in *The eBay Millionaire*. Both of these sellers have built million-dollar businesses by selling similarly sized items.

Strategy Six: Explore All Selling Formats

Until recently, I had sold only through auctions on eBay. In this latest venture, I also sell through an eBay store and occasionally the fixed-price format to capture a greater share of business. Some buyers prefer the immediacy of buying an item through a Buy It Now sale. Others like bidding for a bargain. I want to appeal to all types of customers.

Because I'm selling multiple quantities of the same item in some cases, it made sense for me to open an eBay store. At The Style Channel by Amy (http://stores.ebay.com/The-Style-Channel-by-Amy), shoppers can find an array of products that can be purchased with one click, as well as links to all of my ongoing auctions.

I generally list the same item for auction with a starting bid of 99 cents, while using a higher price at my eBay store. The auctions help drive traffic to the store, where prices are fixed and my profit margins are higher. (It's much cheaper to list an item for sale in your eBay store than in an auction, but auction items are more prominently displayed in eBay search results.)

In my experience, many customers first discover me through my eBay auctions, and the auctions often entice them to buy more products from me through my eBay store. Having an eBay store has proven to be quite profitable, and I would certainly recommend it to anyone selling merchandise in quantity.

Strategy Seven: Do Market Research

Connie Gray of Estate Treasure by Byrum puts particular emphasis on market research. When selling on eBay, it's important to know how much demand exists for your products and the average market price for these goods.

One easy way to suss that out is to use either Marketplace Research, which is available through eBay, or a third-party research tool that looks at past eBay sales data. I subscribe to Marketplace Research and use it every time I create a new listing. The data help me to determine my opening bid price, my Buy It Now price, and even my shipping and handling fee. I try to undercut the competition by a few dollars to make my items more attractive to bidders. Without tools such as this, I'd have no way of knowing how to price products for sale on eBay. You can't look to retail pricing for a cue of how to price in an auction environment. Items are only worth what people on eBay are willing to pay for them.

Strategy Eight: Automate

Time management is crucial to success on eBay. Many inexperienced and amateur sellers waste too much time on repetitive tasks. That takes away from their profitability. (When you're selling on eBay, don't forget to take into account how much your time is worth. The hours I spend on my eBay business are hours I can't spend on writing, which pays me very well, or with my young son, time that's even more valuable than money.) The way to avoid this pitfall is to find ways to automate everything you possibly can.

Using auction management software is one way to make your eBay operation more efficient. I use Turbo Lister, free software that is available for download from eBay, and later Blackthorne Pro, subscription-based software from eBay, to keep track of my entire inventory and to create all my auction ads. Within these programs, I have created templates that include basic item information, my shipping policies, and other routine data. When I want to list a new item for sale, I just have to plug in specific product photos and details.

On eBay, I use Selling Manager to bulk-edit listings, when necessary, and to send out a batch of invoices and e-mails to bidders rather than handling each task individually. Any time I can accomplish multiple tasks at once through automation, I do.

I also use PayPal or the U.S. Postal Service web sites to prepare my shipments for mailing. In the past, I used to type (or handwrite) individual labels for my outgoing packages. Now I use a batch process to create them all at once in a fraction of the time. I've also eliminated daily trips to the post office. Instead, I have the packages picked up daily by the mail carrier for no additional cost to my customers or to me. (Doing so probably saves me an hour or more daily, and that bolsters my profitability because I can spend that time on more lucrative endeavors, such as posting more items for sale.)

Strategy Nine: Focus on Brand Names

I'm doing a lot of things better during this go-round on eBay. But that's not the only reason that I've been so successful. A good deal of it has to do with the fact that I found the right product mix and that I almost exclusively offer brand-name cosmetics, jewelry, and accessories from famous makers including Elizabeth Arden, Lagos, John Hardy, Coach, Kate Spade, and Rolex.

EBay began as a collectibles marketplace, and some very hardworking people, including Connie Gray, have been able to maintain long-running, successful businesses selling antiques, collectibles, and other knicknacks. But the easiest path to riches on eBay by far comes from selling brand-name merchandise. That's the strategy being employed by Amy Mayer and Ellen Navarro of ExpressDrop, a chain of Chicago-based eBay drop-off stores.

As you know, eBay is a very crowded marketplace, with literally millions of merchandise listings. Shoppers usually must use very specific search terms to narrow down their selection. Many type brand names into eBay's search engine to find what they are looking for. So, if you're selling brand-name merchandise, as I am, there's a greater chance that a wide audience of eBay customers will see your products.

Strategy Ten: Provide Superior Service

Consumers have high expectations, whether they're buying from a traditional bricks-and-mortar retailer, from an online store, or through an eBay auction. If you can meet or exceed those expectations, you're going to do much better than your competitors who don't put such an emphasis on customer service.

Your responsiveness to customers and your shipping speed are two important components of superior service. Customers will also pay attention to how you handle your mistakes and their complaints. I'm hardly perfect, and in the course of selling on eBay I've made several mistakes that could have cost me customers. But I've followed the example of eBay's best and have managed to turn these potentially negative experiences into positives for my customers and for my business.

I'll share just a few examples with you. These are things that could happen to any eBay seller, even the most conscientious. Recently, I shipped the wrong size bottle of perfume to a customer. When she alerted me to the error, I immediately sent out a replacement and told her to keep the other bottle with my apologies. My response merited me a positive feedback rating from that customer, in which she called me a "credit to eBay."

Another time, a customer wrote to tell me that she was disappointed with some lotion she purchased from me. She reported that the perfumed lotion had lost its scent, something I had no way of confirming. But I didn't want the customer to be dissatisfied, so I promised to send her a replacement. Unfortunately, I no longer had that particular product in inventory. Not wanting to disappoint her, I went to a local department store and purchased some replacement lotion. I lost money on that sale, for sure, but I preserved my 100 percent positive feedback rating and increased the likelihood that customer will buy from me in the future. The money I spent on the replacement lotion was a small price to pay, indeed.

Here's one final customer-service story of which I'm quite proud. A week or so before Christmas, a customer purchased a product from me that she intended to give as a gift. By the time her electronic check cleared through PayPal, it was too late to ensure holiday delivery with standard shipping. But I knew that the customer needed the package in time for Christmas, so I paid a few dollars extra for guaranteed holiday delivery. The buyer was quite surprised by this gesture and thanked me for it in her feedback.

There's one other thing that I do to deliver superior service, and I can thank Jacob North of Sophias Style Boutique for the idea. As you read earlier in this book, Sophias products come prettily wrapped in tissue paper, as if they were purchased at an upscale boutique. Like North and his colleagues at Sophias Style Boutique, I decided to take a cue from traditional retailers. I sell mainly name-brand cosmetics, which are traditionally sold in department stores. It's not uncommon for the beauty counters at these stores to offer gifts with purchase to encourage people to buy more. Often, when a customer buys multiple items from me, I'll throw in a little freebie as a thank-you. (I always include a handwritten note, as well, explaining that I appreciate their business and want to thank them with a small gift.) Doing so generates incredible customer goodwill, but it also helps serve another purpose: I set aside slow-moving products or items that I have a glut of as free gifts. This actually saves me money because I can easily get rid of my unwanted inventory without having to list it for sale over and over again on eBay.

I'm excited about the turn my eBay business has taken of late, and I owe my success to the Titanium PowerSellers and members of The eBay Billionaires' Club who have so graciously shared their stories and their business practices with me in my books. Through hundreds of hours of interviews with the site's most successful merchants, I've had the unique opportunity to learn from the masters of eBay.

And you have that opportunity, as well. My books collectively contain hundreds of strategies that you can implement to improve your own eBay business. Let the experiences of these Web-based entrepreneurial superstars be your guide to prosperity. Their strategies can work for you, just as they've worked for me, thus putting you on the path to eBay greatness.

Here's wishing you millions of dollars and billions of bids in your online venture!

RESOURCES

Networking Groups for Online Sellers

Internet Merchants Association
www.imamerchant.org

Professional eBay Sellers Alliance (PeSA)
www.gopesa.org

Channel Management and Automation Software

Andale
www.andale.com

Auction Wizard 2000
www.auctionwizard2000.com

Blackthorne Pro
http://pages.ebay.com/blackthorne/pro.html

ChannelAdvisor
www.channeladvisor.com

ChannelMax
www.channelmax.net

eBay Developers Program
http://developer.ebay.com

Infopia
www.infopia.com

Kyozou
www.kyozou.com

Marketworks
www.marketworks.com

Meridian
www.noblespirit.com

Monsoon
www.monsoonworks.com

SellerEngine
www.sellerengine.com

Seller's Assistant Pro
www.ebay.com

SpareDollar
www.sparedollar.com

Truition
www.truition.net

Turbo Lister
www.ebay.com

Vendio
www.vendio.com

Zoovy
www.zoovy.com

Online Payment and Payment-Processing Companies

Google Checkout
http://checkout.google.com

PayPal
www.paypal.com

eBay Research Tools

Andale
www.andale.com

DeepAnalysis by HammerTap
www.hammertap.com

eBay Marketplace Research
http://pages.ebay.com/marketplace_research/

Terapeak
www.terapeak.com

Bidder and Seller Verification Services

BizRate
http://merchant.shopzilla.com/oa/customer_ratings/

BuySafe
www.buysafe.com

SquareTrade
www.squaretrade.com

Shipping Partners and Services

DHL SmartMail
www.globalmail.com

FedEx
www.fedex.com

UPS
www.ups.com

U.S. Postal Service
www.usps.com

Required Reading

AuctionBytes newsletter for auction sellers
www.auctionbytes.com

The eBay Millionaire
www.TheOnlineMillionaire.com

The Online Millionaire
www.TheOnlineMillionaire.com

ACKNOWLEDGMENTS

More than any of my previous books, writing this one was a team effort. Without the help of my friends, family, colleagues, and the featured eBay superstars, this how-to guide would not exist because the deadline coincided with the birth of my first child, Jackson.

Rachel Walden, a young woman who possesses maturity and a work ethic beyond her years, was my second-in-command on this project. She helped me go through hours of interviews and edit them into the text you see in these pages. Ubiqus also provided additional transcription help. And even my husband, Bruce Buchanan, pitched in to get this manuscript completed on deadline. (Thank you, Bruce, for letting me dictate to you, both in words and in demands about household chores.)

My gratitude, as well, to Kirk Kazanjian of Literary Productions and all those at publisher John Wiley & Sons who gave me flexibility in both deadline and format. I also appreciate all the hard work of the copyeditors, page designers, and graphic artists who worked to transform *The eBay Billionaires' Club* from a manuscript into such a handsome volume.

Finally, I want to thank all those people who helped me to manage the other facets of my life and business while I was writing: Mom and Dad (Betsy and Bob Joyner), Linda Edgerton, Aulica Rutland, and Margaret Bell. Thanks for pitching in to help with household chores, other writing projects, and maintaining my sanity.

A. J.

INDEX